The Flying Dutchman and Other Folktales from the Netherlands

World Folklore Advisory Board

THE FLYING DUTCHMAN

and Other Folktales from the Netherlands

Theo Meder

Illustrations by Minke Priester

World Folklore Series

LIBRARIES UNLIMITED

U N L I M I T E D

A Member of the Greenwood Publishing Group

Westport, Connecticut • London

Library of Congress Cataloging-in-Publication Data

Meder, Theo.
  The flying Dutchman and other folktales from the Netherlands / Theo Meder ; illustrations
  by Minke Priester.
    p. cm. — (World folklore series)
  Includes bibliographical references and index.
    ISBN-13: 978–1–59158–490–2 (alk. paper)
  1. Tales—Netherlands. 2. Flying Dutchman. I. Title.
  GR181.M43 2008
  398.209492–dc22   2007022723

British Library Cataloguing in Publication Data is available.

Library of Congress Catalog Card Number: 2007022723
ISBN-13: 978–1–59158–490–2

First published in 2008

Libraries Unlimited, 88 Post Road West, Westport, CT 06881
A Member of the Greenwood Publishing Group, Inc.
www.lu.com

Printed in the United States of America

The paper used in this book complies with the
Permanent Paper Standard issued by the National
Information Standards Organization (Z39.48–1984).

10   9   8   7   6   5   4   3   2   1

The publisher has done its best to make sure the instructions and/or recipes in this book are correct.
However, users should apply judgment and experience when preparing recipes, especially parents
and teachers working with young people. The publisher accepts no responsibility for the outcome of
any recipe included in this volume.

CONTENTS

Part 3: Religious Tales

Part 4: Realistic Tales

Part 5: Tales of the Stupid Devil or Ogre

Part 6: Traditional Legends

Part 7: Contemporary Legends

Part 8: Riddles and Puzzles

Part 9: Anecdotes and Jokes

Part 10: Formula Tales

INTRODUCTION

Dutch History and Outlook

There is a rather small country in Western Europe that is not so much the land of the brave, as it is a home of the free.

Beyond its successes in farming and fishing, it has been a nation of sober-minded dike-builders and seafarers, priests and ministers, traders and painters. The country is called the Netherlands, mainly because almost half of the land lies below sea level and needs to be protected by dunes and dikes. The other name for the country, Holland,[1] actually refers to the two most prosperous provinces (North Holland and South Holland) in the west. The Dutch share the problem of being partly below sea level with their southern neighbours the Belgians, and that's why both states are sometimes referred to as The Low Countries. Then there is the language that the Netherlands and Flanders (the northern part of Belgium) have in common; in this entire region, Dutch has become the standard language of the people. The one exception is the Frisians, in the north of the Netherlands, who speak Frisian, a language related to English as well as Dutch and German. The Frisians are probably the earliest inhabitants of the Netherlands and are not related to Germanic tribes that invaded the land later on, like the Batavians, Caninefates, and Angles, although their languages must have influenced each other. Celtic influence in the Netherlands has been speculated on but never proven.

The Netherlands is surrounded by three large and mighty nations: Germany to the east, France to the south, and England to the west. During the Middle Ages the Netherlands was never a sovereign state, but always consisted of a number of counties and duchies belonging to the German empire, the kingdom of France, Burgundy, or Spain. Oppression during the Spanish military occupation, from the sixteenth century onwards, was considered harsh and ultimately led to the Dutch rebellion for freedom. During this period the northern part of The Low Countries had turned Protestant and desperately longed for religious freedom; many Protestants from the south fled to the north to avoid the death penalty for being "heretics." Viceroy William of Orange (1533–1584) led the struggle of the northern Dutch provinces against Spain, but he never saw the end of it. The war lasted from 1568 to 1648, but William of Orange was killed by the French Catholic traitor Balthasar Gerards in Delft in 1584. Previously this war against Spain was called the Eighty-Years War, but today it is seen as a fight for freedom, and the Dutch prefer to call it the Rebellion. After the Dutch provinces gained their freedom in 1648, more provinces joined the union.

William of Orange (aka William the Silent)

The seventeenth century was the Dutch golden age—an era of seafaring, discoveries, colonization, and trade. In the east and the west the Netherlands founded colonies, for instance Indonesia, Surinam, and the Antilles. In 1602 the VOC (United East-Indian Company) was founded, and it made the nation rich through the trade in tea, coffee, tobacco, and all sorts of spices. It must be noted that during this time the Dutch were notorious slave traders as well, transporting many Africans to the plantations of the West Indies and the American mainland.

Until well into the eighteenth century, the Netherlands was governed by viceroys and state representatives in parliament. Sympathy was felt for the French Revolution of 1789, which turned France into a republic and propagated the ideals of *"liberté, egalité et fraternité"* ("freedom, equality, and brotherhood") . Soon after Napoleon Bonaparte took control of France, French troops occupied the Netherlands. The Netherlands became a kingdom for the first time, with Emperor Napoleon's brother Louis as king from 1806 onwards. After Napoleon's defeat in 1815, the Dutch Orangist party took power and installed William I of Orange, eldest son of viceroy William V, as king. The Netherlands has basically remained a kingdom since then (see chart, below). A united kingdom with Flanders only lasted fifteen years; in 1830 the Flemish separated from the Dutch.

King William I (1815–1840)
King William II (1840–1849)
King William III (1849–1890)
Queen Emma (1890–1898), regent for Wilhelmina
Queen Wilhelmina (1890–1948)
Queen Juliana (1948–1980)
Queen Beatrix (1980–today)
King William-Alexander (heir to the throne)

Kings and queens of the Netherlands

Although the Netherlands managed to remain neutral during the First World War, the country was occupied by German troops in the Second World War (1940–1945). The bombing of the inner city of Rotterdam; the plundering of many Dutch resources; and the deportation and annihilation of many Jews, resistance fighters, homosexuals, and gypsies have left behind a lingering, silent resentment towards the Germans within the Dutch population. The Netherlands was liberated by mainly American and Canadian Allied troops. Every year the Dutch commemorate the war victims on May 4, and celebrate Liberation Day on May 5.

The former Dutch colony of Indonesia gained its independence in 1949, followed by Surinam in 1975. The Dutch Antilles are still part of the kingdom.

For a long time the Netherlands had eleven provinces: Friesland, Groningen, Drente, Overijssel, Gelderland, Utrecht, North Holland, South Holland, Zeeland, North Brabant, and Limburg. In the twentieth century the sea called Zuiderzee was turned into a lake called the IJsselmeer, by building a long dam between North Holland and Friesland (1932). Within the IJsselmeer, land has been reclaimed from the water, and it officially became the twelfth province in 1985, called Flevoland. The ancient island of Urk has now changed from the province of Overijssel to Flevoland.

Outside the Dutch Parliament in The Hague. Photo by Theo Meder

Nowadays some 16 million people live in the Netherlands, of which Amsterdam is the capital, while the government resides in The Hague. The two southern provinces, North Brabant and Limburg, are Catholic; the northern provinces are mainly Protestant. However, since the 1960s church attendance has been diminishing. In addition, as a result of the immigration of Turkish and Moroccan labourers and their families, a million Muslims now live in the Netherlands, especially in the four largest cities: Amsterdam, Rotterdam, The Hague, and Utrecht. Compared to other countries, the largest Dutch cities are still relatively small; in 2006, for instance, Amsterdam had only about 750,000 inhabitants.

In foreign countries the Dutch have the reputation of being cheap and stingy. Foreigners who speak a little Dutch say, "Kijken, kijken, niet kopen," which means, "just looking, not buying." Certainly the Dutch are always on the lookout for bargains, and tradesmen are known to buy cheap and sell at considerable profit.

For several centuries the Dutch have also had a reputation for political and religious tolerance, as well as for liberality where trade, drugs, (homo)sexuality, euthanasia, and abortion are concerned. The Dutch are not particularly patriotic, militaristic, or proud of their own history or cultural heritage. Unlike, for instance, American culture, Dutch culture has few historical heroes; perhaps that's why the Americans invented Hans Brinker for the Dutch. The only outbursts of Dutch patriotism occur during matches of the Orange national soccer team.

Equality is highly valued in Dutch society; feelings of superiority are considered to be a vice, and so most of the time boss and employer, and even teacher and pupil, call each other by their first names. Being ordinary is a virtue. One of the most famous sayings in the Netherlands is, "Doe maar gewoon, dan doe je al gek genoeg," meaning, "Act normal, that's crazy enough already." Another striking example of contemporary Dutch mentality is the need to be authentic, "gewoon jezelf zijn" (that is, just being yourself), not pretending to be someone else or playing some kind of role.

Finally, the Dutch have a vivid and straightforward sense of humor, as well as a flourishing culture of stand-up comedy, called "cabaret." Thanks to this sturdy and direct sense of humour, the Dutch are able to put things in (Dutch) perspective, ridiculing the unwise and unmasking the pompous.

Dutch Feasts, Dishes, Snacks, and Sweets

Many of the Dutch feast days (holidays) are international, such as Easter, Mother's Day and Father's Day, Christmas, and New Year's. One of the rituals during Easter is the painting, hiding, and eating of eggs, especially when there are children around. A traditional snack eaten on New Year's eve is "oliebollen," crispy balls of dough, raisins, and currants, fried in oil and covered with powdered sugar. The end of the old year and the coming of a new one are celebrated with fireworks at midnight. A newly invented tradition is to take a bath in the cold North Sea at Scheveningen (or elsewhere) on New Year's morning.

Recently a tendency has arisen to take over American celebrations like Valentine's Day and Halloween as well. Halloween is mainly celebrated amongst adolescents, who dress up in scary clothes, while the children's trick-or-treat routine more or less belongs to the newly restored feast of Saint Martin (November 11). In the evening children go from door to door with their Chinese lanterns to sing "Sinte Maarten" songs and collect candy.

Two typical Dutch and national festivals are Queen's Day and Saint Nicolas ("Sinterklaas"). Queen's Day is still celebrated on the birthday of the late Queen Juliana (April 30). Nowadays Queen Beatrix visits two cities in the Netherlands, which organize a festive program in her honour. All the inner cities array themselves in orange, and the main attractions are the flea markets, accompanied by (live) music, food, and drinks. A traditional liquor consumed on Queen's Day is "oranjebitter."

At the end of the twentieth century the Dutch began to fear that the international Father Christmas or Santa Claus was going to dominate and suppress their own feast of Saint Nicolas or Sinterklaas (December 5). After nationwide protests, the feast was restored to its former glory. It all starts in November, when Sinterklaas—dressed as a bishop—and his black servants—all called "Zwarte Piet" (i.e., Black Peter)—arrive in the Netherlands by steamboat from Spain. Welcomed by the mayor and many young children, Sinterklaas mounts his white horse, Amerigo, and along with all the Black Peters he goes to prepare for December 5, when he will give all the children (and most adults) in the Netherlands poems, sweets, and surprise gifts. It is said that on the eve of December 5 he rides over the rooftops, while the Black Peters descend through the chimneys to distribute the gifts. In order to please Sinterklaas, before they go to bed the children sing "Sint Nicolas" songs and leave their shoes near the chimney, often with a winter carrot and some water for Amerigo. Every once in a while there is discussion about the figure of Black Peter, because he particularly reminds us of our past involvement in black slavery; it has been argued that we should have Green, Orange, and Blue Peters as well, to avoid any suggestion of racism. The feast of Sinterklaas has his own kind of sweets, including "speculaaspoppen" and "taaitaai" (both gingerbread figures), "pepernoten" and "kruidnoten" (gingerbread nuts), "suikerbeesten" (marzipan animals), chocolate mice and frogs with a soft marzipan filling, and chocolate letters.

Other regional festivities are "carnaval" (carnival, Mardi Gras) and the "Elf Stedentocht" (Eleven Cities Tour). The real carnival is celebrated in the southern Catholic provinces of North Brabant and Limburg. It starts a few days before Ash Wednesday and Lent. In these days, the cities get carnivalesque names (for instance, 's-Hertogenbosch becomes Oeteldonk) and are ruled by carnival princes. People dress up as farmers, monks, pirates, etc., and every city hosts a procession with floats, often mocking local affairs and politics. Live music and a lot of dancing and beer drinking go on during carnival.

The Eleven Cities Tour is traditional Frisian, and can only be organized during severe winters, when the ice is thick enough to successfully support this skating tour. The almost 200-kilometre (125-mile) long tour goes from Leeuwarden to Sneek, IJlst, Sloten, Stavoren, Hindeloopen, Workum, Bolsward, Harlingen, Franeker, and Dokkum, then back to Leeuwarden again. In the second half of the twentieth century, only six "Elfstedentochten" could be organized (winners: 1954, Jeen van den Berg; 1956, no winner; 1963, Reinier Paping; 1985, Evert van Benthem; 1986, Evert van Benthem; and 1997, Henk Angenent). The "pro-

---

fessionals" are allowed to start first, after which the "amateurs" may attempt to win a medal for completing the tour. Nowadays the "professionals" are able to finish within seven hours. Along the way, crowds and small orchestras cheer for the contestants. Favourite drinks during cold winter tours are hot chocolate and Frisian Beerenburg (gin with a herbal extract).

A traditional Dutch dish, favoured by young and old throughout the country, is "pannenkoeken" (Dutch pancakes). They are baked in a frying pan and are much flatter and crispier than American pancakes. Following is a recipe.

Pannenkoeken (Dutch Pancakes)

Ingredients:
250 grammes (approx. 1 cup + 5 tsp) self-rising flour
salt
0.5 litre (approx. 2 cups) milk
butter
1 egg
sugar or syrup (made of cane sugar)

Directions:
1. Put the flour in a bowl.
2. Make a small hole in the middle, break the egg into it, and add 2 decilitre (¾ cup) milk. Add a pinch of salt.
3. Mix to combine, gradually adding the rest of the milk, until the batter is smooth and without lumps.
4. Melt butter in a frying pan over high heat.
5. Pour approximately ½ cup batter into the frying pan for each pancake and fry on each side until brown.

Makes approximately 8 pancakes.

Serve the pancakes with sugar or syrup on top.

These pancakes are often rolled up and eaten with a knife and fork. Special pancakes can be made by putting bacon or cheese in the pan before adding the batter.

Traditional Dutch dishes are heavy soups and stews, fit for hard-working farmers to nourish and warm the body. In most cases, the stews consist of vegetables mashed with potatoes, such as "boerenkool met worst" (kale hotchpotch with smoked sausage), "hutspot" (a stew of carrots, onions, potatoes, and bacon), "hachée" (potatoes, onions, and beef), and "zuurkool met worst" (sauerkraut and potatoes with smoked sausage). Traditionally, the soups are rich and nourishing as well, such as "erwtensoep" (pea soup), often served with rye bread and cheese. Modern Dutch society has grown accustomed to other cuisines as well, such as French, Indonesian, Italian, and Moroccan. Today we can also buy fast food at McDonald's, Burger King, Kentucky Fried Chicken, and Pizza Hut.

Dutch pancakes, plain and with bacon and cheese. Photos by Theo Meder

When Dutch people are abroad for too long, they start craving typical Dutch snacks and sweets. One of our favourite sweets is "drop" (a sweet or salty black licorice), which is difficult to obtain elsewhere. Peanut butter and chocolate sprinkles are favourite Dutch sandwich fillings. There is some Dutch fast food from our own "snack bars": Dutch fries with mayonnaise, "kroketten," and "bitterballen" (the latter both meaty ragout snacks in a crispy fried layer). Raw (new or green) herring, sprinkled with bits of onion, is considered a delicacy by the Dutch; traditionally, it has been consumed by tilting one's head back and lowering the fish, with the tail between thumb and forefinger, into one's mouth.

Frozen and fried "bitterballen." Photos by Mereie de Jong

Preferred drinks in the Netherlands are coffee, tea, milk, and buttermilk. The traditional alcoholic Dutch drinks are beer (with Heineken the most famous brand) and "jenever" (gin). The Dutch today have learned to appreciate wine as well. Youngsters drink a lot of soft drinks, and our adolescents have discovered the cocktail-like "breezers."

Dutch Narrative Culture

Like any other European country, the Netherlands has a rich narrative culture, in the past as well as in the present. Many of the traditional folktales, like fairy tales and legends, have been collected from oral tradition since the nineteenth century or are found in even older literature. Fairy tales like "Little Red Riding Hood," "Snow White," "Cinderella," "Bluebeard," and "Sleeping Beauty" are well known in the Netherlands, although here one might suspect literary influence from Charles Perrault and the Grimm Brothers (and more recently Walt Disney). That's the main reason why in the past Dutch folktale collectors hardly bothered to take these stories down from oral tradition. Most of the collectors were looking for "authentic" oral tales among the farmers and fishermen, who supposedly had lived in isolation from any literary culture for centuries. Apart from fairy tales, many legends have been recorded, about mermaids, giants, gnomes, witches, sorcerers, werewolves, and hauntings. Particularly in the southern Catholic provinces, many legends about saints and holy objects (crucifixes, hosts, statues, and images) have been found as well.

The collecting of folktales in the Netherlands started some time after the Brothers Grimm published their *Kinder- und Hausmärchen* in Germany in the early nineteenth century. At first Dutch scholars thought fairy tales were too insignificant to study. Starting in the mid-nineteenth century, local folklorists collected tales in their own regions, especially where the local language and culture were supposed to be threatened by more dominant ones: Flanders, Limburg, and Friesland. At the end of the nineteenth century philologist and folklorist Gerrit Jacob Boekenoogen (1868–1930) took up the task of collecting folktales on a national scale. He used the same methods the Brothers Grimm had: He went looking for tales in archives and old books and asked people from all over the country to send him letters with folktales and folksongs, originating from oral tradition. In this way he obtained a lot of unique material. One of his correspondents proved to be a true fieldworker; rural physician Cornelis Bakker (1863–1933) from Broek in Waterland (North Holland) interviewed many of his patients—mainly dairy farmers, farm hands, milkmen, and fishermen—with remarkable results. One of Bakker's best storytellers was local dairy farmer Dirk Schuurman (1839–1908), who had several tales in his repertoire that have never been found since in the Netherlands, such as "The Taming of the Shrew" (belonging to an ancient and international tradition that had inspired William Shakespeare as well).

G. J. Boekenoogen

C. Bakker

Unfortunately, for many years Boekenoogen's collection remained unpublished (until the twenty-first century), and his life's work did not result in any serious academic incorporation of the study of folklore in the Netherlands. Over the years, only a handful of scholars took an interest in Dutch folk narrative, and fieldwork and collecting tales were left to local folklorists again. In the 1960s and 1970s the documentation and research institute that is today called the Meertens Instituut (part of the Royal Academy of Arts and Sciences) started a program to collect folktales on a national scale again. The main objective was to obtain legends and folk beliefs from all over the country, to facilitate the drawing of folkloristic maps. After a while, more than twenty collectors were allowed to take down fairy tales and jokes, too. Altogether they collected some 30,000 folktales, more than half of which were collected by one man, the Frisian collector and assistant minister Adam Aukes Jaarsma (1914–1991). Well after World War II, Jaarsma was still able to find storytellers, like the Frisian mole catcher and smallholder Anders Bijma (1890–1977), who were able to tell the traditional fairy tales from the oral tradition.

In 2006 the Meertens Instituut created a professional centre for preserving, collecting, and researching Dutch folktales, called DOC Volksverhaal (Documentation and Research Centre for Folktales). Among other things, the DOC Volksverhaal is responsible for maintaining a Dutch Folktale Database, with more than 35,000 narratives in it (www.verhalenbank.nl).

A. A. Jaarsma

A frequently asked question is, "Are there any typically Dutch folktales?" The honest answer is no, not really. The Netherlands is a small country, right at the intersection of Germanic and Romance culture, and folktales from both cultures can be found here in abundance. Furthermore, Dutch society is receptive to many stories. In fact, almost all folktales by nature consist of international narrative material; there are no boundaries for good stories, and that's why folklorists are able to make international catalogues of folktales.

Of course, in a way a tale is typically a Dutch tale when told in the Dutch or Frisian language or in some Dutch dialect; language is an important marker of identity. In quite a lot of Dutch folktales I find some kind of social comment, expressing sympathy for the underdog, the common man, and the principle of equality and liberty, as well as distrust towards authority and heroism. Maybe one could say that typical of many Dutch tales is that they are about farmers and fishermen, about cows and pigs, about polders (land recovered from water) and—above all—about water, water, and even more water. This is not surprising for a country near the sea, with many lakes, rivers, brooks, canals, and ditches—with more names for waterways than the English language can provide. (We think that there is a difference between a "kanaal," a "singel," and a "gracht," yet they are all called a "canal" in English.)

So isn't that story of Hans Brinker, the famous boy with his finger in the dike, a Dutch story *par excellence*? No, it isn't. The tale was invented by the American writer Mary Elizabeth Mapes Dodge (1831–1905) and was told in her children's novel *Hans Brinker or the Silver Skates*, dating from 1865. By the way, Hans Brinker is the hero of the novel, but *not* the boy with his finger in the dike. This boy only appears in a story read in school, and he remains anonymous. Although Dodge claims the legend is known by everyone in the Netherlands, it was completely unknown over here before she wrote it down. With all the water and the dikes and the flooding, the story could have been Dutch, if the boy weren't such an American type of hero. As mentioned previously, the Dutch don't like heroes that much. Nevertheless, I gave the story a place in this book ("Hansie Brinkers of Spaarndam") because whether we like it or not, the boy has become a Dutch icon, thanks to the many American tourists who visited our country after World War II. We even erected a little statue of "Hans Brinker" in Spaarndam in 1950 to please the tourists. ("Dedicated to our youth, to honor the boy who symbolizes the perpetual struggle of Holland against the water.")

As examples of genuine Dutch tales about water, flooding, and drowning, I have included legends such as "Here Is the Time," "The Mermaid of Westenschouwen," "The Mermaid of Edam," "Childrensdike," "The Herring in the Bucket," and "The Fall of Tidde Winnenga." All of these Dutch legends are a bit gloomy, as legends should be, for there is seldom a happy ending in legends. All somehow deal with the topics of destiny, fate, doom, and misfortune, and the acknowledgement that man is powerless against these forces. Furthermore, the legends confirm that the water and the sea can give and take, and that every once in a while there is room for a small miracle. Hardly any heroes can be found in Dutch legends, but victims can be found in abundance. If the victims are innocent, we sympathize. If the victims are guilty . . . serves them right! Incidentally, the legend of "The Flying Dutchman" isn't originally Dutch either, because the tale started as a literary tradition in England.

There are two exceptions in this book to my statement that there are no "authentic Dutch tales"; the tale of the apple-catching test ("The Soldier of Barrahuis") and the urban legend "The Wandering Comforter" are probably originally Dutch. At least, it looks like the centre of origin was the Netherlands.

Dutch narrative culture does not only consist of traditional fairy tales and legends. There are modern jokes and urban or contemporary legends, too. In Dutch the latter genre is called "broodje-aapverhaal" (monkey-burger story), after the title of the first Dutch book published on the subject by Ethel Portnoy (1927–2004). Because modern jokes and legends are as much a part of our cultural heritage as the traditional genres, I was compelled to include them as well. I even added some stories that came to the Netherlands with immigrants from Surinam, the Antilles, and Turkey. After all, our present-day society has become a multicultural one.

Currently the Dutch make jokes about these same immigrants, and the different immigrant groups make jokes about each other as well. The Dutch don't make jokes about their British or French neighbours, only about the Belgians and the Germans. The jokes about the Belgians are reasonably friendly; the Belgians are only supposed to be a bit backward. In the jokes about the Germans ancient hostilities can be found: The Germans are perceived as militaristic, loud, rude, and humourless. New trends in humour are imported from the United States, just as easily as the contemporary legends are. We have our share of dumb blonde jokes—and the wave of lawyer jokes is likely yet to come (as soon as our lawyers take over the American vulture culture).

I would like to add a warning here: This collection contains a wide range of tales, but not every story may be suitable for every reader. Therefore educators and parents should always review any particular story before sharing it with children.

The order in which the folktales are presented here is mainly inspired by the folktale catalogues of Uther (2004), Van der Kooi (1984), Sinninghe (1943), and Brunvand (1994); see "Sources and Further Reading."

Contemporary Dutch Diversity and Dynamics

Many tourists come to the Netherlands expecting to see Dutch stereotypes like wooden shoes, tulips, and Gouda cheese. Of course, if they visit the right tourist traps, they will actually see these things. In reality, few farmers wear wooden shoes any more. The tulip is not an indigenous Dutch flower; we imported the bulbs from the Turks who—in their turn—obtained them from the East. Dutch strengths were importing, cultivating, and selling again. We still like to manufacture and eat Gouda cheese, but the transport is by truck, boat, and plane, not the funny-dressed men the tourists see at the "cheese market" in Gouda.

Surely the Netherlands is a country of windmills, bicycles, painters like Rembrandt and Vermeer, and the so-called Deltawerken. The old pittoresk windmills, once used for grinding, pumping, and sawing, have become protected monuments. Every new windmill we build is slim and white and very high and for the production of electricity only. The Deltawerken is an ingenious twentieth-century project of dams, dikes, dunes, and sluices to keep the North Sea out. Most flooding nowadays occurs not when there is a break in the dike, but when rivers take too much rain and meltwater to our delta. How about that, Hans Brinker?

The Netherlands is a country with modern art and architecture as well. Not only were Rembrandt and Vincent van Gogh born in the Netherlands, but also Jeroen Bosch, with his gruesome "End of Days" paintings, and Karel Appel, with his abstract compositions. In Dutch society the use of soft drugs like marijuana and hashish has been legalized, as well as prostitution, same-sex marriage, abortion, and euthanasia. On the other hand, firearms are hard to come by—Dutch citizens are more concerned about violence than about (adult) love and sex, so to speak.

Dutch society is diverse and dynamic, and these same features can be found in Dutch culture and narratives. Actually, it is impossible to speak of *the* Dutch culture, because there are so many different groups with their own (sub)cultures and their own narrative repertoires. Men tell different tales than women, seniors tell different stories than adolescents, Christians tell different tales than Muslims, businessmen tell different stories than goths, Antilleans tell different tales than Turks, and so on. Looking for features, values, and narratives that all Dutch have in common will—of course—lead to generalizations.

For a long time the Dutch were barely aware of our shared values and own identity. After the terrorist attacks of September 11, 2001, the sense that Western culture was being threatened grew, and we started contemplating who we were and what we stood for. Along with a growing consciousness of our own moral values, roots, and identity, interest in Dutch historical and cultural riches increased, leading to the conviction that our own intangible heritage (like narrative culture) should be cherished and preserved.

Although it may be hard to believe, there is no ever-present fear of flooding in the Netherlands these days. We hardly give a thought to the fact that most of us live below sea level—we don't feel threatened by it. This is probably the best way to avoid eternal depression. Our history and narrative culture prove that we are not constantly on the brink of drowning, but—on the contrary—have managed to keep our feet dry most of the time.

Notes

1. Probably from "Holt-land," which means woodland.

THE NETHERLANDS

Part 1

ANIMAL TALES

WHY BEARS HAVE SHORT TAILS

*I*t happened in the wintertime when everything was covered with snow and ice and there was hardly anything to eat for all the animals.

One day, the bear and the fox met each other and the bear asked: "How can you be so merry in these times of hardship? I am starving, and you look as if there is no famine at all."

"That's right," the fox answered, "My belly is full of food. I have been fishing and I have eaten as much flounder as I wanted."

"Listen," the bear said, "you must teach me how to fish, because I'm so hungry, I could eat a horse."

"That can be done," the fox replied, and he brought the bear to a place with a little hole in the ice.

"Look," he said, "this is my fishpond. Put your tail through the hole and the fish will hang on to it, and as soon as the load is heavy enough, just raise your tail again and you'll have more fish than you can possibly eat."

That's worth a try, the bear thought, and he stuck his beautiful tail through the hole in the ice and waited until the fish started to bite.

After he had sat there for quite a while, he asked the fox: "Do you think I have waited long enough?"

"I don't think so," the fox replied: "You'll have to wait a little longer."

The fox made the bear wait for so long that his tail froze to the ice and could not be pulled out anymore.

Then he laughed at the bear and said: "Pull harder! Your catch must be heavy."

The bear pulled as hard as he could, but to no avail.

In a final attempt, he pulled so hard, that his tail snapped off. Since that time bears have very short tails.

This animal tale is known as folktale type ATU 2, *The Tail-Fisher*, and was collected around 1900 by G. J. Boekenoogen (1868–1930) in the Zaanstreek (North Holland). The translation is based on G. J. Boekenoogen, "Nederlandsche sprookjes en vertelsels," *Volkskunde* 15 (1903): 114–115.

THE FOX AND THE WOLF

*O*nce upon a time the fox and the wolf stole six small barrels of butter from a farmer, and they immediately emptied two of them. They hid the remaining four barrels. The hiding place was far away from their homes, though. Soon the fox worked up an appetite to eat from another barrel by his own, but to be able to undertake the journey, he needed to go and borrow the boots of the wolf. Upon being asked what his intentions were, the fox answered that he had to attend the baptism of a child, which would get the name *For Starters*. Soon, the fox came to borrow the boots for a second time. A second child had to be baptized, which would receive the name *Halfway the Barrel*. Later on, a third child was called *Down the Barrel,* and a fourth *Scratch the Bottom*.

Some time later, the fox and the wolf decided to go to the barrels together. The fox had been clever enough to fill up the empty barrels with stones again and spread out a thin layer of butter on top of them. The fox and the wolf started to quarrel about who was allowed to eat first, so they decided to draw straws, and the wolf won the first bite. Naturally, he only got a mouth full of stones, and they accused each other of having emptied the barrels.

On the journey back, they saw an old horse sitting in a ditch. They wanted to take the animal home. They decided to tie the tail of the horse around the waist of the wolf, so the wolf could pull, while the fox would hit the horse with a twig. So it happened. The horse got released from the ditch, but now he started running with the wolf on his tail.

"Thump your heels in the ground!" the fox yelled.

"Are you kidding? I can hardly distinguish heaven from earth!" was the answer.

Finally, the wolf got free again, and both animals continued their way back home. As they came home, the wolf sat down with his back to the fire, because he was soaking wet. Sitting like that, he soon fell asleep. Immediately the fox went for a small piece of butter and smeared it under the tail of the wolf. Due to the heat, the butter started melting soon, and the fox woke the wolf with the remark that now it was for everyone to see who had emptied the barrels.

This fable is a version of ATU 15, *The Theft of Food by Playing Godfather*, as well as ATU 47A, *The Fox Hangs onto the Horse's Tail*. The story was sent to collector G. J. Boekenoogen on August 28, 1894, by J. O Hazekamp, who lived in Eenrum (province of Groningen), but was born in Beilen (Drente). The translation is based on T. Meder and C. Hendriks, *Vertelcultuur in Nederland* (Amsterdam, 2005), pp. 156–157.

THE LION'S SHARE

*T*he lion, the fox, and the donkey went hunting together. They managed to catch a lot of game.

The lion said to the donkey: "You must divide the catch."

So the donkey divided all the game into three equal parts.

However, the lion is the king of the animals, and what the donkey had done did not please him at all. He got angry, grabbed the donkey, and tore him to pieces.

Then he said to the fox: "Now you divide the catch."

The fox was sly. He threw all the game on one big heap. Then he humbly begged the lion for a small bite.

Hereupon the lion granted him more meat than he was ever able to eat.

This short fable is a version of ATU 51, *The Lion's Share*. The tale was told on May 19, 1966, to collector A. A. Jaarsma by the Frisian storyteller and mole catcher Anders Bijma, from Boelenslaan. The translation from Frisian is based on T. Meder, *De magische vlucht* (Amsterdam, 2000), p. 29.

THE WOLF AND THE GOAT

A mother-goat went to the wild
And warned her only little child
To keep the door locked very tight
And keep the fearful wolf outside.
A wolf came by and tried to fake
The sounds a mother-goat would make.
The goat looked through a hole he knew
And said, "You scoundrel, I know you!
Why did you make the sound you made?
May God's dishonor be your fate!"
So never will you end up dead
If you obey your mom and dad.

This is a thirteenth-century verse version of ATU 123, *The Wolf and the Kids*, written down in the Middle Dutch manuscript of fables called *Esopet*. The translation is based on G. Stuiveling, ed., *Esopet* (Amsterdam, 1965), part 2, p. 39.

THE HISTORY OF OLD-BOVETJE

*O*nce upon a time there was a man called Old-Bovetje. He had a lot of children to take care of. He was afraid of the wolf, and so were his children. One day Old-Bovetje urgently had to go out, and he feared that, while he was away, the wolf would come and eat his children. After all, that was what the wolf would love to do. Old-Bovetje decided to hide all of his children very well, so that the wolf would be unable to find them. He put one on the table, one under the table, one on the chimney, one under the chimney, one in the box bed,* one under the box bed, one on the chair, one under the chair, one in the cooking pot, one on the cooking pot, one on the milk jug, one in the milk jug, and one under the milk jug. All in all, the children were hidden extremely well.

Now Old-Bovetje said to his children: "If the wolf comes knocking on the door, calling 'Little children, little children, open up!', don't open the door. Reply: 'I am afraid to, because the wolf will b-b-bite me.' Will you promise me that?"

"Yes, Old-Bovetje!" all the children yelled, "we promise."

"Fine," Old-Bovetje said, "good-bye then, my little children!"

"Good-bye, Old-Bovetje," the children said, and Old-Bovetje went out.

The children all sat there quietly and did not dare to move an inch, although particularly the young boy in the milk jug and the little girl under the cooking pot were extremely short of breath. They sincerely hoped that the wolf would not come, but sure enough, after ten minutes, they heard knocking on the door—a very loud knock on the door—and a deep wolf's voice howling: "Little children, little children, open uh-up!"

The children were scared stiff.

Finally, the one in the milk jug answered: "I am af-f-fraid to, because the wolf will b-b-bite me."

The wolf repeated his awful howling three more times and the children repeated their answer, because they didn't want to be bitten by the wolf.

In the end, the wolf got fed up with this game—he had a lot of things to do that afternoon, and this whole matter had lasted too long to suit him. He took a little run up and blew with all his might. The door—as if out of sheer terror—burst open with a tremendous bang.

The wolf entered and ate all the children, even the one in the milk jug. Of course, this meal made the wolf extremely fat—so fat that he could barely button up his overcoat.

All of a sudden, Old-Bovetje returned home. In one quick glance he understood what had happened and shouted: "Where, where are my little children?"

Nobody answered.

"You ate them all, didn't you?" Old-Bovetje said to the wolf, "yes, I can tell you did."

Then Old-Bovetje took a large knife that was lying on the table and cut the belly of the wolf open. One after another the children hopped out, cheerful, alive, and well. What a joy that was! Old-Bovetje embraced them all, and he gave the wolf needle and thread to stitch up his belly again. The wolf left and never returned again, while Old-Bovetje and all of his children lived happily ever after. This now, is the true history of Old-Bovetje.

---

*A traditional Dutch bed built in the wall that can be secured with wooden doors.

Another version of ATU 123, *The Wolf and the Kids*, this time from the nineteenth century. The story was sent to collector G. J. Boekenoogen (1868–1930) in January 1894 by novelist Cornélie A. Noordwal (1869–1928) from The Hague (South Holland); she remembered the story being told by her grandfather. The translation is based on T. Meder and C. Hendriks, *Vertelcultuur in Nederland* (Amsterdam, 2005), pp. 227–229.

THE DOG AND THE SPARROW

*O*nce upon a time there were a dog and a sparrow who went out walking as friends. After they had walked for a while, they got hungry. As they approached a farm, they made up a plan: The sparrow would fly in and untie the knot holding the bacon hanging in the chimney, whereas the dog would jump over the back door and catch the bacon under the chimney.

They agreed to follow the plan. When the dog arrived at the fireplace, he saw that there was a spinning woman present and that there was porridge cooking in a pot near the fire. The woman threw a stone, but instead of hitting the dog she broke a piece of the pot. The dog didn't want to leave before the bacon had fallen. Finally, the bacon came down, and the dog jumped over the back door again with the bacon in his mouth.

Together they lay down in a cart track and ate. The sparrow said that the dog could eat as much as he liked. The dog ate too much and was unable to leave the cart track again.

Then the farmer came speeding down the track in his wagon. The sparrow cried: "Don't run over my pal."

Alas, the farmer did not listen to the sparrow and ran the dog over, so that his insides splattered out of his body. The dog was killed instantly. The sparrow was so mad that he sat down on the head of the farmer's best horse and pecked out an eye. The angry farmer tried to kill the sparrow, but to his embarrassment he killed the horse instead. As the farmer walked home, the sparrow followed him right into the farmhouse. Inside, the farmer said to the sparrow: "I wish I could catch you."

Then the sparrow said: "Place a trap over there on the cupboard. I will fly into it."

Soon the sparrow flew into the trap and the farmer got hold of him and said: "I am so mad that I don't know what to do with you."

The sparrow replied: "Eat me up alive."

So the farmer ate him up alive.

After a while, the farmer had to go to relieve himself, and he ordered his wife to observe if the sparrow would come out again.

His wife took a look and said: "Here he comes." The woman took an axe and asked: "Do you want me to chop?"

"Yes," the farmer replied.

The axe came down and . . . the sparrow withdrew himself a bit and the wife chopped off a slice of her husband's bottom.

Then the sparrow flew away, saying: "Now you have lost a piece of your porridge pot, your best horse is dead, and there is a slice of your rear end. Serves you right!"

This animal tale is known as folktale type ATU 248, *The Dog and the Sparrow*. The story was recorded in 1804 by eleven-year-old Gerrit Arends Arends (1793–1876) from Ezinge (Groningen). The storyteller was Trijntje Wijbrands-Alberts (1749–1814), an old seamstress with the nickname Trijntje Soldaats (because her first husband was a German soldier). The tale is one of the few in which the sympathy is with the animals rather than the people. The translation is based on J. van der Kooi, *Van Janmaanje en Keudeldoemke* (Groningen, 2003), pp. 162–163.

WHY THE BEANS HAVE BLACK SPOTS

*O*nce upon a time there were a straw, a burning coal, and a bean. They went out for a walk together. After they had walked quite a distance, they were suddenly confronted with a ditch. They did not know how to cross the water, because the ditch was too wide to jump over.

Finally the straw said: "I've got a good idea. If I lay myself over the ditch, the coal and the bean can alternately walk over me to the other side. Then you can both pull me to the other side, and then we can walk on." So it happened. The straw lay itself over the ditch, the bean waited on the one side, while the coal walked over to the other side. However, once the coal was in the middle, the straw started burning and they both fell into the water. When the bean saw this, he started laughing so hard that his belly burst.

The bean went to a blacksmith, who repaired the burst with a little black plate. Now the bean was mended again, but until today you can still see that every bean has a little black spot.

This story is a version of ATU 295, *The Bean (Mouse), the Straw, and the Coal.* The tale was sent to collector G. J. Boekenoogen in April 1894 by Mrs. J. ter Meulen from Tiel (Gelderland). The translation is based on T. Meder and C. Hendriks, *Vertelcultuur in Nederland* (Amsterdam, 2005), pp. 216–217.

ANANSI THE SPIDER

A long time ago, Anansi the spider used to live in Africa, but along with the slaves he moved to Surinam and the Antilles. Not so long ago he moved to the Netherlands, and he decided to go and live under the roof of a Dutch windmill near the centre of Utrecht.

Anansi was a little lazy by nature, so most of the time he had nothing to eat and no money at all. However, if you want to live in the Netherlands, you need to have a lot of money. Being an African spider, he did not care much for money, but thanks to his cleverness he was always able to survive.

One day, Anansi went to the hunter and said: "Hunter, my wife is ill, and I can't afford to buy the proper medicine. Would you lend me a hundred guilders?* I will pay you back in three months."

Next, Anansi went to the tiger. "Tiger, my dear, dear tiger! My wife and all of my children are ill. Can't you lend me a hundred guilders for a while? I will pay you back in three months."

Then Anansi went to the rooster. "My dear, dear, dear, dear rooster. My wife and my children turned terribly ill. I can't afford to pay for their medicine any more. I have been thrown out of the national health insurance** because I failed to pay my premium. Please, give me a hundred guilders, and you'll get it back in three months."

Finally, he went to pay a visit to the beetle and asked him to lend a hundred guilders for his sick family as well.

Indeed, after three months, it looked like Anansi was going to pay off his debts.

He went to the beetle first. "Come to my place at four o' clock this afternoon, and I will pay you back the hundred guilders I borrowed from you."

Then he visited the rooster. "Come to my house at a little past four o' clock this afternoon, and I'll pay you back your hundred guilders."

Next, he went to the tiger. "Come to my place at a quarter past four, because I still owe you a hundred guilders."

Finally, he went to the hunter. "I still owe you a hundred guilders. Come to my place at—let's say—twenty past four, and I will pay you back."

Before his guests arrived, he put a large washtub full of water under a tree, next to the windmill.

Exactly at four o' clock the beetle arrived.

"My dear beetle. Come and have a seat. Yes, I want to thank you very much for lending me those hundred guilders. I was in such dire need. My entire family was . . . . Gee, what a coincidence: here comes the rooster."

"The rooster?!"

"Uh, you can hide behind the door."

The beetle hid behind the door.

"Ah, my dear rooster. Come sit for a while. Yes, I really need to thank you for the hundred guilders you lent me. You know, my family was so incredibly ill, we were so poor and without that hundred guilders of yours . . . . Well, what do you know! What a coincidence. Look over there; here comes the tiger."

"The tiger?!"

"You better hide behind the door."

The rooster hid behind the door, saw the beetle, and "peck," he swallowed him down at once.

"My dear, dear tiger. I am so pleased that you are here, because I want to wholeheartedly thank you again for the hundred guilders you lent me three months ago. Please, have a seat."

"No, I don't want to. I want my money."

"Oh, alright then, uh . . . . I'll get it for you. Meanwhile, I have a little present for you, behind the door. Go and have a look, while I get the money."

Anansi went up into the windmill. The tiger looked behind the door and saw a fat, juicy rooster sitting over there. So he opened his mouth real wide and swallowed the rooster in one bite.

Just as Anansi wanted to give the tiger his money back, he looked out with surprise and said to the tiger: "Well, look over there! Here comes the hunter."

"The hunter?!"

"Quick, tiger, climb in that tree."

The tiger climbed the tree and reached the top in one huge leap.

Meanwhile, Anansi offered the hunter a chair. "Yes, I wanted to express my gratitude again for the hundred guilders you . . . . Oh dear, hunter, what incredibly dirty feet you have! Why don't you go wash them? Under the tree over there, you'll find a washtub full of water."

The hunter walked to the washtub, and just as he was about to put his feet into the water, he noticed the reflection of the tiger. He went for his rifle and shot the tiger out of the tree. Bang!!

Anansi, who had gone inside to get the money, came running out again after hearing the gunshot.

"What did you do? That was the king's tiger! He was staying at my place to learn the Dutch language. If I tell the king that you shot his tiger, you'll be put in prison."

"Please, Anansi, don't tell the king. Uh . . . . I will give you a hundred guilders and then uh . . . . We'll think of something."

"Well, alright then," Anansi said, "I'll tell the king that the tiger passed away during his lessons, and that I have already buried him."

The grateful hunter paid Anansi a hundred guilders and he was even prepared to dig a grave.

When the hole was deep enough, Anansi said: "You know what? Just go home now. I will put the corpse in later and fill up the grave for you."

As soon as the hunter had left, Anansi took his knife and skinned the tiger. The leftovers went into the grave and he filled the hole very nicely. Problem solved. That is to say . . . . Anansi got rid of his debts, received a hundred guilders extra, and from the hide of the tiger he could make a fur coat for the winter. A real nice coat . . . .

*The guilder (Dutch, *gulden*) was the common currency in the Netherlands until the introduction of the euro in 2002.

**Insurance for medical and dental care for people with lower incomes, provided by the Dutch state.

This (unpublished and slightly reworked) Anansi tale was told to me on November 5, 2000, by the Dutch professional storyteller Raymond den Boestert in Utrecht (province of Utrecht). As a result of immigration from Surinam and the Antilles during the late twentieth century, stories about Anansi the spider are becoming increasingly popular in the Netherlands.

Part 2

TALES OF MAGIC

BLUEBEARD

*B*luebeard insured his wife for a lot of money. After that, he tickled her under her feet for so long that she died.

His second wife was insured for a high amount of money again. After she died, he threw her in the cellar.

With his third wife he did exactly the same.

All together he had seven wives, and he burned their corpses in a round iron stove for heating.

However, he got caught when he attempted to burn the seventh woman in the stove. He immediately committed suicide by hanging himself.

This very short and peculiar Bluebeard tale is a version of ATU 312, *Maiden-Killer* (*Bluebeard*). The story was told to collector A. A. Jaarsma on August 18, 1966, by the Frisian storyteller, mole catcher, and smallholder Anders Bijma (1890–1977). It was not unusual for Bijma to—deliberately—tell his own deviant versions of well-known stories (see Venbrux and Meder, 1999). The story, here translated from Frisian, has not been published before (archives and Folktale Database, Meertens Instituut, Amsterdam).

THE CHOCOLATE HOUSE

*O*nce upon a time in a large forest, there lived a poor lumberjack with his wife and two children, named Stoffel and Elsje. Winter had been severe that year, leaving the father little to earn. To add to their misfortune, he became very ill and died. Now his poor wife was left with her two children. Not much had remained of their savings; only just enough to keep them from poverty for a while. One day in spring—a cold, bleak day it was—the mother, being herself somewhat ill, was forced to send both her children into the forest to gather some wood, so that she could cook their dinner. The children obeyed willingly and went on their way.

At that time, Elsje was seven years old and Stoffel was six years of age. When they had finished gathering wood, they went home, but no matter which way they walked, they could no longer find the house. They were lost. Then they both began to weep. Elsje put the bundles of wood on the ground and took her little brother by the hand to try to find their way back once more. Finally they saw a cottage in the distance, which they decided to approach. They thought, "There might be good people living there who will take us back to our mother." How surprised they were when they came to the house and saw that it was entirely made of chocolate and that the little windows were made of sugar. Since they had not had anything to eat since that morning, they had become very hungry. They assumed nobody was living in the house and since they could not hear anybody either, they began to break bits of chocolate off the house and eat them.

Just when they were very engaged with this, they heard a shrill woman's voice from inside calling:

> *Who's nibbling on my house?*
> *Surely 'tis a little mouse.*

She opened the chocolate door and came out, with her knitting in her hands. A grey cat followed her and an ugly owl sat on her shoulder. She was an old, ugly, skinny, bony, wrinkly, tawny woman—dressed in a floral pattern garment made of wool. And on her head she was wearing a big brown hat under which some grey hairs became visible. The witch had large, ugly, green eyes, overshadowed by bushy, grey eyebrows, a hairy, protruding chin, a long, pointed, black-spotted nose, and an amazingly large mouth with two long, crooked teeth sticking out on either side. Terrified, the children wanted to run away.

The ugly woman, however, called to them in a friendly manner: "Fear me not, dear little children, I will do you no harm."

The children turned around and Elsje said that they were lost and longed for their mother.

Whereupon the witch replied: "I will give you something to eat first."

Encouraged by the witch's friendly words, the children followed her inside. In the house, there was a clear fire burning in the hearth, with a large kettle of food over it. The children sat down at the chocolate table, drank from sugar cups, and ate from sugar plates. They had had such a delicious meal, which had been so nourishing for them, that they were well able to face a night at the cottage, at the witch's request. After all, it was becoming too late and too dark to return to their mother that day. They got a nice feather bed each and slept more comfortably than ever before.

The next day, after having had a hearty breakfast, they thanked the woman for her cordial reception and also asked her to take them back to their mother. The woman answered their question, announcing that she was a witch, and that they could never leave the place again now that they had come to her. The children began to weep bitterly.

The witch said, "Weeping won't do you any good here! Now be silent and if you will always be obedient, you will have an agreeable and pleasant life here. If not, I will change the both of you into animals."

The last thing she said made such a great impression on the children that they stopped weeping. From now on, Elsje had to help the witch with her work. Stoffel was allowed to play, for the time being, until he was older. Every morning, the witch had to fetch water from the well at the back of the house. After the children had been there for three days, the witch ordered Elsje to come along with her to draw water—the witch intended to throw both children into the well; first Elsje, then Stoffel. But Elsje could not draw water, so the witch showed her how to do it. Due to the woman's impatience, though, she bent too far forward, fell into the well, and drowned. Although she was shocked by what had happened, Elsje was very glad. She freed Stoffel from the house and then they walked home.

In the meantime, the mother was in great fear when her children did not return. Every day, she went to a hill in the woods to have a better look around. On the third day she was back on the hill, she saw her children coming towards her. Full of joy, they embraced each other and Elsje told her everything.

The following day, they went to the house, and after some investigation, they found the witch's treasures in the cellar. All of a sudden, they were immensely rich. They bought a beautiful house with lovely lands, and they all lived happily ever after.

Then there was a pig with a long snout, which blew the entire story out.*

---

*One of the traditional Dutch formulas to end a fairy tale (the pig can be an elephant as well).

This fairy tale is a version of ATU 327A, *Hansel and Gretel*. The tale was sent to collector G. J. Boekenoogen on June 20, 1892, by Mrs. M.R van der Veer from Driebergen (Utrecht). The translation is based on T. Meder, *De magische vlucht* (Amsterdam, 2000), pp. 51–53.

THE OLD HAG

*O*nce upon a time there lived a king and a queen. Every single day, the queen went to a large forest to pray.

One day, an old woman came up to her and asked, "What brings you here?"

"Oh, sweet woman, I am willing to tell you, but you will not be able to help me. I have been married for so long now and I would very much like to have a baby boy."

"Well," said the old woman, "things are not so bad. I think I will be able to help you. Here you have a little bean. Make sure you plant it in a flowerpot in your house and return to this place to pray every day."

And so the queen did. Little less than a year later, she had a beautiful, sweet baby boy.

"But," the old woman in the forest said the last time she came there, "never must you allow the child to walk outside on his own. It is best to keep him inside the house at all times. Because if he walks outside without you, some great harm will be done to him. You must keep him with you until he is twelve years old."

The queen took very good care of her son until he was as old as eleven years. At that time, the king gave a large hunting party for the young noblemen in the neighbourhood. These gentlemen were very anxious to take along the young prince on their hunt.

They begged for so long and promised to take care of him so well that the king said, "Well, things have been going so well for such a long time that I expect them to go equally well from now on. Take him along with you, but be careful with him."

The young prince shot a large deer himself, but did not kill it immediately. The deer ran into the forest. The prince went after it, but the chase took so long that evening had fallen when the prince discovered that he was lost in a large forest. The deer had disappeared into the bushes and the prince stood there alone. He climbed a hill with a large tree on it, but since he had never learned to climb trees, he used the height of the hill to take as good a look around as possible. In the distance he saw a light coming from a small house, which he approached.

An old woman answered his knocking on the door, and when he had told her everything, she said, "Do come in. You are allowed to spend the night here, if you are prepared to run an errand for me tomorrow."

The prince said very cheerfully, "I'd be delighted to."

He thought he might have to go into town to get some stocking wool or other such things. But oh dear, he couldn't have been more wrong. In the hut, there were also three blonde girls, who called the old woman "mother." The oldest girl was very friendly to the prince and helped him with everything, took him some hot milk, and helped him upstairs to his little room, where he slept comfortably the whole night through. The prince was in a good mood. This sweet girl, he thought, will surely show me the way out of the forest.

The old woman appeared and said, "Well, here's the errand. Here you've got a small wooden axe. I will go to the forest with you. You will have to chop down the entire forest today, and if you won't finish it today, I will cut your head off."

The prince thought, my head will surely come off then, for I do not even know how to chop, let alone with a wooden axe.

When the old woman had left, he started weeping from fear and shock.

In the afternoon, the sweet girl came to bring him some food and said, "You'll be tired enough as it is from yesterday's walking. Just go and have a lie down, and I will wake you up in time."

The girl had secretly taken the old woman's magic wand—the old woman actually being an old hag—and used it to make all the trees fall down, except one.

"There you are," she said when she woke up the prince, "now make sure you chop away on that one tree when the hag comes around tonight to check your work. She kidnapped all three of us, and we don't have the courage to run away."

When the girl returned home in the evening, the old hag went to the forest and took her along.

She then said to the prince, "You have been very diligent indeed. You are now allowed to marry this sweet girl. You must now use this wood to build a large house for the both of you to live in."

"Oh," said the prince, "I'm not capable of doing that."

"Well, you'd better make sure to find a way to do it; after all, you have also done a neat job chopping the wood. And if you can't do it, I suppose your head will have to come off anyway."

The girl nudged him behind the hag's back.

"Just you wait," she whispered, "I still have the magic wand. I will help you."

And indeed, the next day the entire house was finished, complete with doors and windows, cupboards and closets, tables and chairs, and curtains for the beds. The day after, they got married. All of a sudden, they heard someone calling, and recognized the hag's voice.

She called out: "Are you asleep already?"

"No, not yet!"

The hag waited a while until they would be asleep, but the girl said, "Let's get dressed silently."

They knotted the bed curtains together and tied them to the knob of the window. They then lowered themselves out the window by the curtains and ran off as fast as they could.

Once more the hag called out, "Are you asleep already?"

And when she heard no reply, she went in and cut crosswise through the bed with a large knife. If they had still been lying in it, they would have been slaughtered and killed. The following day, the hag went to the new house and saw, arriving at the cupboard bedstead, that they had already left it and that she had only slashed the blankets. This made her furious.

Back home, the hag told her husband, "You are a fast walker, go and get them back quickly."

The husband went after them. Just when he thought he saw something in the distance, they both noticed him. The girl rapidly transformed both of them into flowers by a tap with the magic wand. The hag's husband was just about to grab hold of them when he saw that he had definitely made a mistake, because he had only seen some flowers. He went home and told all of this to his wife.

The hag said, "If only you had picked those flowers; it was them! Go back quickly and bring along everything you see which you think could be them, because it *will* be them."

The husband walked as fast as he could (because this man had also been kidnapped and was equally frightened of her). But the flowers were gone and he no longer saw them. Finally he thought he saw them.

But the girl saw him too and turned herself into a church with a pulpit. She told the prince, "I will change you into a minister. Make sure you do a good job preaching on the pulpit."

"Oh," said the prince, "I don't know how to preach; what must I say?"

All of a sudden, the man saw that he had not seen things properly—that the thing he had seen was a church.

He went inside the church and heard the clergyman say three times, "It will be Sunday tomorrow!"

Well, the man thought, that is some minister. I could preach the way he does. Does he think I don't know that myself?

He slammed the church door behind him and went home to tell the hag everything.

"Oh," said the hag, "you are a fool, you are good for nothing; that was them!"

The man said: "You can hardly expect me to bring along this entire church."

"All right," said the hag, "just you be careful I won't transform you into a church. I'll go after them myself. Then you'll see how soon I can lay my hands on them."

She did not give herself time to tighten her hat or look for her magic wand. Instead, she rushed out of the house and into the forest, just like that. A long way from home, she arrived at a lake. The girl had seen her coming and had changed herself into a lake and the prince into a duckling.

She told the prince, "Now make sure you stay right in the middle, and no matter how hard she tries to lure you, don't go ashore, because then we'll be lost. I am now much more frightened than when the man came."

When the hag arrived at the water, the duckling stayed nicely in the middle, and no matter how many pieces of bread she threw to entice the little animal, it did not come.

Just you wait, she thought, you won't fool me. I know it is you. Upon my word, I am tired and hot from walking and I am very thirsty. Then she began to drink the water, she sighed and groaned, but kept drinking. She could hardly breathe . . . but still she continued drinking. She had nearly finished it all; the duckling was swimming around in a very small puddle indeed.

When the hag felt she could drink no more, and that she would soon burst, she called out, "Just you come here, this is the end of me. Look, I am bursting and dying. Take this little box; it may come in handy some day."

And then she was dead. The prince and the girl walked for a very long time, until they arrived at the king's palace.

Before they arrived there, the girl said to the prince, "You must not let anybody kiss you, because then you would no longer recognize me. After all, I am your wife and would like to keep it that way after all we've been through."

"No," said the prince, "I will take good care of that."

She said, "And I will make sure I'll find a position as a servant. You just stay with your dad, and we'll be able to see each other every now and then. But don't tell them you are married to a maid."

The girl hired herself out to a miller and the prince arrived at the palace. When he came there, everybody started to kiss him and embrace him and there was joy all over now that the prince had returned. The following day, the queen gave a very large feast in honour of the prince. The entire neighbourhood was invited, because everyone, both rich and poor, had assisted in the search when the prince had disappeared during the hunt. The miller also prepared for the feast and got dressed in his best suit.

The girl said to him, "I wouldn't mind coming along."

"I'm sure you wouldn't," said the miller, "but you can't."

"Please, I am so looking forward to it."

"I am sure you are, but you don't have any pretty clothes and you can't possibly go in these working clothes."

"Just you wait," she said, "I do have pretty clothes."

Back in her small room, she tapped on the little box with her magic wand and behold! A magnificent gown issued from it.

At the feast, she was much better dressed than the queen and she herself was a ravishingly beautiful girl.

The queen asked her if she could have the gown. She then said, "Yes you can, provided I can spend one night here in the palace."

"Of course you can," said the queen.

So when all was quiet, she went to the prince, but he did not remember her, nor did he recognize her, because he had allowed his mother and all his aunts to kiss him.

"But oh," she exclaimed, "I am your sweet wife. Surely you must remember me?"

In the morning, the girl returned to the miller. That evening, there would be another large feast, and the miller would go there again too.

The girl said, "I would love to come along once more."

"I'm sure you would, but you've lost your gown now. What can you do?"

"Well," said the girl, "that is no impediment."

She now appeared at the feast in an even more beautiful gown.

The queen was enraptured. "Oh," she said, "do give me that!"

"All right," the girl said, "provided I can stay here again tonight."

"Sure," said the queen, "the presence of a lady with such good taste is highly encouraged in our court."

The girl went to the prince and talked to him.

He was beginning to pay more attention now. The old king was hiding in the closet, because the courtiers had informed him that their guest went to see the prince. In this way, the king heard everything they were discussing.

"Oh," said the girl, "don't you remember anything of all the things that went on in the forest, and of how I helped you and how this hag kept trying to catch us until all this water made her burst?"

"Yes," said the prince, "I remember everything now, and how good and sweet you've been to me, and how much we all owe you. But what should I tell my father?"

"Well," said the girl, "tell your daddy that you have two rings. One of loveliness and one of unloveliness; which one shall I dispose of? You'd better do as your father tells you."

The king in the closet found it very sweet of the girl to teach and tell the prince to obey his father. When the prince was asleep, the king silently got out of the closet. The following morning, the prince told him everything.

The king said, "You must dispose of the ring of unloveliness and retain the other one. That will surely make us all happy. I heard everything last night and we will all love your wife very much."

The king told the queen, and they had six horses harnessed to a carriage to fetch the miller's maid, who rapidly issued another magnificent gown from the hag's box before she got on the carriage. That very same day, they got married solemnly at the town hall and in the church, and in the evening, there was a great ball and they all lived happily ever after.

This fairy tale is a version of ATU 313, *The Magic Flight*. The tale was sent to collector G. J. Boekenoogen on January 22, 1894, by Mrs. S. H. Junius from Arnhem (Gelderland). The translation is based on T. Meder, *De magische vlucht* (Amsterdam, 2000), pp. 45–51.

Part 2: Tales of Magic

BERTHA AND THE SEVEN MONKEYS

*O*nce upon a time there was a mother, who had a stepdaughter and a daughter of her own. Her own daughter was a malicious girl, whereas her stepdaughter was a virtuous girl. One day, the good girl, whose name was Bertha, had to get water from the well. As she arrived at the well, there was an old woman sitting on the edge who asked her for something to drink.

Bertha was very kind and gave her something to drink, whereupon the old woman said, "You're such a good girl. I am a fairy. Today, if you go home, rubies, pearls, and other precious stones will come from your mouth with every word you speak."

Immediately after she had spoken, the fairy vanished into thin air.

When Bertha went home, her stepmother was angry because she had not returned at once. Now Bertha told of the old woman, and with every word diamonds and pearls fell from her mouth.

The next day, the mother said to her angry daughter Anna, "Today you have to get water and obtain the same valuables as a reward."

Anna wasn't used to chores like getting water, and she left in a bad mood.

This time, there was a distinguished looking lady sitting near the well and she said, "You girl, give me something to drink."

Anna, unaware of the fact that this was the same fairy, got angry and replied, "If you want something to drink, get it yourself!"

"Phooey, what a nasty girl you are," the fairy said. "With every word you speak, toads, worms, and other such vermin will come from your mouth."

When she got home, her mother said, "Now speak, and show me those treasures."

Anna, however, was angry and tried to speak as little as possible, but after a while all kinds of nasty vermin left her mouth anyway.

Then the stepmother exclaimed that Bertha was to blame for it all, and she chased her off into the woods. Poor Bertha got lost, and as it became dark, she saw the light of a little house in the distance. The door was open. She called, but there was no one home. There were dirty plates and leftovers on the table. She was hungry, so she took some food. Next, she neatly cleaned the dishes.

There were seven beds. She made them up, and then started to clean up the whole house. Finally, she cooked soup for the next day and went up to the small attic to sleep, because she was exhausted.

Some time later seven monkeys came home. One exclaimed, "How tidy has this place become!" Another said, "How excellent does this soup taste!" And a third said, "How soft does my bed feel!"

Then they went to sleep, and Bertha quietly left the house again.

The next morning the seven monkeys woke up, and they searched the house for the person who had tidied up their place so well, but they couldn't find anybody. They said, "Whoever did this must certainly be a virtuous girl, fit to marry a prince."

Since she was tired, Bertha had fallen asleep in the woods again. The fairy touched her, and she became as beautiful as a princess.

A prince, who happened to be hunting in the woods, found her and instantly fell in love with her.

Bertha woke up, and the prince asked her to follow him to the court and marry him. The prince obtained the approval of the king and queen. And so they married and lived happily ever after.

This fairy tale is the only combination of ATU 403, *The Black and the White Bride,* and ATU 709, *Snow White,* ever found in the Netherlands. At the end of the nineteenth century it was sent to collector G. J. Boekenoogen by A. Veenhuyzen, an elderly physician from Alkmaar (North Holland). The translation is based on T. Meder and C. Hendriks, *Vertelcultuur in Nederland* (Amsterdam, 2005), pp. 342–343.

ROZINA

*I*n a trading town in France there once lived a wealthy merchant—a widower—with three daughters. The two eldest, Louise, aged eighteen, and Irma, aged seventeen, were spitting images of their deceased mother. They were highly vain, selfish, stingy, and idle. The youngest was a fifteen-year-old girl named Rozina. She exceeded both her less good-looking sisters by her extraordinary beauty. She had a slender, graceful figure, long blond curls, clear, friendly blue eyes, a small mouth, enclosed by coral-red lips, and teeth as white as pearls. However, she excelled more for her charm than by her beauty. Like her father, she was gentle, modest, diligent, and good to all people, particularly to those in need. Therefore, she was better loved by her father and by the people who associated with her than were her sisters. Now this grieved her elder sisters much. Consequently, they treated Rozina in an ever-disdainful manner and laughed at her piety, which they called hypocrisy, and always teased her in all sort of ways. The poor girl bore all this patiently and hoped to change and reform them by means of her goodness.

One day the father was going on a business trip and asked each of the girls what gift he should bring back with him. Louise wanted a silk dress and Irma asked for a velvet cloak bordered with fur.

"And what shall I bring you, Rozina?"

"Oh father, I have no need for anything, but if you wish to give me something anyway, then I'd prefer a rose, my favorite flower, which doesn't bloom here anymore. You may be able to obtain one yonder."

The father cordially said good-bye to his daughters and left. After a week, his business was done and so he bought the silk and velvet garments. But he could not get a rose anymore. On his return to town—still by stage coach in those days—he asked to be taken to the large forest near town. He thereupon left the coach and went through the wood on foot. It was still early and very light and not any later than five o' clock in the afternoon. Deep in thought, he did not notice having lost the main road, which led straight to town. Instead, he had taken a side road, which went deep into the wood. Only now did he become aware of it, but he could no longer find the main road and was lost. There in front of him, he discerned a

---

wonderful, majestic white marble magic palace amidst vast flower gardens and parks, in which ponds were rippling, fountains were rising, and enormous white marble statues stood between the tall trees and the bushes. He opened the high iron gate and entered the flower garden. Filled with admiration, he took a rapid glance at everything in passing, climbed the high, wide white marble stairs of the palace, and went through the front gallery to the main gate, which was made of iron and entirely gilded. He knocked, but noone came, and after waiting for a long time, he decided to go in through the gate, which was not locked.

Having gained access, he first entered a large vestibule and after that a large, wide corridor, which were both made out of white marble as well. As in the front gallery, there were many beautiful plants and flowers arranged on either side. He opened a heavy door made of cedar wood and entered a large gilded hall, lavishly furnished and with walls hung with valuable paintings and mirrors. It appeared to be a dining room, although the table was laid for one person only; there were several dishes, conserves, bottles of champagne, etc. Everything he had seen until now seemed very magical to him, and it was just as if he found himself in a paradise on earth here. It puzzled him, though, that no person had appeared yet—he did not even see a magical fairy, to whom he had thought all this must belong. Since he himself had become fatigued and hungry, he sat down and ate with relish. After this, he went to the flower garden to look for roses. After all, it was not any later than six o'clock yet. He walked alongside the pond, in which two beautiful white swans were floating.

In the water there also was an elegant pleasure boat, complete with oars. Over the pond, which was fairly broad, was a bridge. He crossed the bridge and sat down on a bench, which was shaded by tall beech trees. After he had rested, he walked on. He now saw a high rock, in a large pond, from which a waterfall sprang. Moving on, he saw a reservoir with goldfish in it. The park and the flower garden also contained overgrown summer houses and broad, leafy lanes. He went through a lane and arrived at a lake, in which lay a small island with a crystal summer house on it, surrounded by pretty flowerbeds. A small boat, which lay here too, enabled him to row towards the island. He went back the way he had come as soon as night began to fall, even though it was still fairly light, and he noticed that the moon had started to risc. From the park he returned to the flower garden and had a look at the greenhouses, which contained many exotic plants and flowers. He did not have much time left to admire such beauty properly, and while he was thinking again of the rose, he went outside into the garden. Passing many beautiful elegant plant and flower beds, he looked around for roses. He was filled with awe of all the splendour he had seen—even though he had only received a fleeting impression of everything we have just described, from beginning to end. He had not even seen a quarter of the beautiful, vast pleasure gardens. Since there was no time left and he was longing for home, he saw, having arrived at the roses, that there were not many; the ones that were there, though, were of a particularly beautiful kind and of pleasant scents. He picked a large, beautiful rose. But no sooner had he picked it and was holding it in his hand, than he heard a terrible roar and saw a black figure from the palace approaching him. When the shape came closer, he saw a most hideous, large monster. Bolted to the ground by shock, the man could not flee from the monster.

When the monster stopped roaring, it said, furiously, "Thou ungrateful creature! Is this a way to behave after having enjoyed so many good things? Why of all things must you pick this beautiful rose of the few I possess? Why do you act like this, you ungrateful one? By way of penalty, you are bound here for life!"

Finally the man, who was still quivering from fear, could utter a word. He fell to his knees before the monster and asked for forgiveness. He confessed why he had picked the rose, to wit, for his daughter Rozina.

When he had confessed everything, the monster replied, "Now that you have made a candid confession, and are repenting it deeply, and also because you had not picked the rose out of ill will, but for someone else, I am prepared to release you. But only on the condition that you, when you return home, send the first member of your family approaching you here to me. This family member must then stay here instead of you, and although this person shall have a good life here, he or she may never leave this place anymore."

The merchant was thinking . . . . Whenever he went on a journey, he was used to being approached first by his faithful dog, and for this reason, he promised to fulfill the promise. When the poor man, recovered from the shock, was back in the wood, he did not see the castle anymore, but noticed in confusion that he was walking on the ordinary, main road to town. Having come close to his home, he saw—to his surprise—that it was not his faithful dog, but his daughter Rozina who approached him first. He turned pale and became very sad. After having embraced him cordially, Rozina asked what was the matter with him and if he had become ill from the trip. The father replied in a friendly manner that he was not ill, but that something unpleasant had happened to him, and that he would talk about it after having rested a bit.

After both the eldest daughters had welcomed their father, they received the fine garments, which exceeded both their expectations because of their beauty and value. Consequently, they both thanked him cordially for the gifts and noticed only now that their father looked so pale and sad, and they also asked about the cause of this. Thereupon, the merchant related everything that had happened to him in the magic palace and then handed the fatal rose to his youngest daughter. She was deeply shocked by the thought that she would have to be separated from her beloved father and spend the rest of her life with a monster, on her own. However, the thought that she could serve as a sacrifice for her dear father, whom she loved so dearly and whose life she would spare—provided she went willingly—prevailed in her good heart. She accepted and was prepared to leave the next evening, although she wept in silence at the thought of the impending separation from her relatives.

The sisters had listened to everything indifferently. They were very surprised about this wonderful, magic palace and the beautiful pleasure gardens, but at the same time, they were very pleased that it had not been one of them that had been forced by fate to remain there forever. They would have wanted to go there only for a day to have a look at everything, but this was all right as well.

The next day, the separation between father and daughter was heartbreaking, and many tears were shed. But the sisters simply said farewell to Rozina and wished that she would well like the solitude. In their hearts, they were even glad that Rozina departed from them, so that they would never again be outshined in their beauty by anyone. Moreover, they would be free to do as they pleased, because their father was too busy with his business to pay much attention to them.

Rozina left sadly, following the same broad lane through the forest that her father had taken. Like him, she suddenly faced the magic palace. She opened the gate and entered, passed through the wonderful flower garden, climbed the white marble stairs, and went through the gallery to the iron gilded gate, then opened it and thus arrived in the same illuminated dining room. She was pleasantly surprised when she saw that all the plates and dishes carried her name, ROZINA, in graceful gold letters, and it puzzled her that her arrival was known here, and also that no monster had appeared yet. She ate of the delicious food and when she had finished, she rested a bit. She heard the clock strike seven. All of a sudden, she heard a roar, like from a bull, through the corridors. Doors were smashed open and finally, the monster reached the dining room door, which was opened. The hideous monster now revealed itself to her gaze. The poor girl was terror-stricken and quivered and wept with fear.

The monster, however, spoke to her in a friendly manner, "Fear not, Rozina, no harm will be done to you. I may be repulsive, but I am not ill-natured. You will surely be fatigued; come with me and I will show you to your bedroom. In order to make you feel at home here, I had already arranged to have your name printed on all the plates and cups, so that you will from now on regard everything you will find here as your own."

Rozina thereupon expressed to the monster that she had found all this very pleasant and thanked him for all his good deeds. She then followed the monster, albeit still with hesitation. It went up the wide white marble stairs. There were densely flowered heavy carpets everywhere, on the stairs and in the hall.

In the hall, the monster opened the gilded door of a bedroom and said, "I hope you will like this room well, Rozina; in it, you will find everything you need for your dress, and I also wish you a good night's sleep."

Then the monster took its leave, after first having put the golden sconce with light in it on the mahogany table. Rozina now looked around the room; she had never seen such a beautiful bedroom, let alone ever possessed one. The wallpaper was gilded; all the furniture, the chairs, and sofas were covered with light blue silk, just like the bed curtains, and the sheets were of fine fabric. The mirror, in which she could see herself from her head to her feet, was large and wide and its frame was solid gold—and the frames of the valuable paintings hanging there were made out of gold, too. She saw another door, which she opened to see that it led into a boudoir. It was entirely covered in pale pink and contained one of the most valuable dressing tables she had ever laid eyes on. There was also a wardrobe; she looked in it and uttered a cry of surprise when she saw wonderful fine garments, which contrasted so sharply with the plain but decent clothes she was wearing. She tried something on. It became her very well. There were also many jewelled ornaments, bracelets, rings, earrings, etc., lying there. Rozina would have thought that all this belonged to a princess, were it not that she knew that all this had been given to her. In the boudoir there was another door, which led into a bathroom. She looked at it and saw that like the other rooms, it contained everything she needed. After having seen and admired everything, she went to bed. She slept well, because she was very fatigued, and she dreamt of goddesses and fairies.

Rozina awoke the following morning and saw that the sun was already shining through the windows. She dressed herself in the valuable garments and went out, and when she left the room, she noticed only now that over the doors of the three rooms, ROZINA could be read in gold letters as well. She pitied the hideous monster and admired his goodness to her. She went downstairs. In the dining room, breakfast was ready, ever so rich and copious. After breakfast, she went into the parks and gardens. Everything she saw here seemed infinitely more beautiful to her than her father had described. After having taken a long walk, resting on a sofa or in a summer house from time to time, she went over to the palace to have a look at it from the inside. The first hall past the dining room was made out of silver with furniture beautifully covered with satin, shining like gold. On the other side there was a hall made of solid gold, including even the floor and the ceiling; here the golden furniture was covered with cherry red velvet. The third hall was shining with diamonds and precious stones. The fourth hall was a dance hall, with small, furnished rooms on the sides, which led back to the ballroom via richly covered sliding panels instead of doors. She passed through many more halls, all of which seemed to compete with each other in valuable furniture, ornaments, paintings, and so on. Finally she arrived in a garden hall made out of crystal, which contained many exotic plants; in the centre there was a reservoir with a fountain in it, which gave off fragrant odours. Rozina dipped her delicate handkerchief into it, and it became so fragrant that all the perfumes in the town were nothing compared to it.

Since it had already become midday, she went back to the dining room. Dinner was ready. To Rozina, it appeared to be a meal fit for a king, there were so many dishes, and conserves, preserves, cakes, desserts, and all sorts of fine wines. The table and all the victuals were decorated with beautiful live flowers, bouquets, flower baskets, and so on. After dinner Rozina went into the park to see the ponds. She wanted to go inside the crystal summer house on the island. Over there, she saw an elegant boat, which carried her name as well. The boat had no oars, but had gold ribbons on the front. Every ribbon had a silver swan drawn on it, which made her understand that she was supposed to hitch the two white swans floating on the water to the boat. And so she did. The animals willingly obeyed, and in a stately manner drew the boat to the island. In her beautiful pale blue silk garments, set with diamonds, with her slender and extraordinary beauty, in the boat with the two swans in front of it, Rozina looked like a wonderful water fairy, floating to her water palace.

When this water excursion was finished, Rozina went to the stables—an equally beautiful, large building. Here she encountered many beautiful breeds of horses and a sweet pony. She thought of a name for this animal and called it out of the stables. It approached her willingly and neighed cheerfully. There were also carriages of all kinds, but one of them was exactly suited for two people and ever so elegant on the front. This carriage was also the most valuable one in the collection, since it was made of gold, inlaid with diamonds. This carriage carried her name as well; the letters were formed by precious stones. Rozina could not admire it enough. She harnessed the snow-white pony to the carriage. It appeared to know the way very well, and Rozina did not have to use a whip. She drove around almost the entire estate, but the evening began to fall and she always made a habit of doing things regularly.

Just as on the previous evening, a rich and copious dinner awaited her. Rozina thought about all the beautiful things she had seen. Indeed, she began to find the surroundings so pleasant, and she enjoyed herself so much, that she would not mind about never being able to return to the human world, if only her father could be here with her, to amuse her and share her solitude. Now that she was here, she decided to make as little use of the precious halls as possible, except of her own rooms. She preferred to find her amusement outdoors. When she could make trips in the carriage or the boat or make other outings, she felt infinitely more free and cheerful than in those magnificent but lonely halls.

The monster only visited her every evening at seven o'clock, so as not to trouble her, and took his leave again when she wished to have a rest. The multitude of gifts with which she was showered had reconciled Rozina entirely to the hideousness of the monster. She also decided to speak to him in a more friendly manner, because she did not want to seem an ungrateful girl. At seven in the evening, the monster arrived as usual. As ever, he spoke to her in a very friendly manner and asked her how she liked her surroundings. Rozina thereupon told the monster about all the wonderful things she had seen. She just could not describe how beautiful everything was to her, and for this reason, she thanked the monster very much for everything.

He replied, "I am very pleased that you like everything so much and that you are enjoying yourself so well here. Rozina, now that you are here, I want you to regard everything as your own, and therefore I appoint you as queen over everything. You will never be short of the most precious garments and jewelry, but in exchange for all this, I would kindly want to ask you something."

"Speak," said the girl, "if possible, I shall be of assistance in the matter."

Thereupon the monster begged, "Rozina, would you be my wife?"

Rozina was unpleasantly surprised by this request, because she had not in the least thought of marrying this hideous monster. Nay! She could not do it; it repelled her. It was indeed very sorrowful to her, having to refuse this request. But she said that she would be prepared to think it over. The monster bade her goodnight and went his way. In this manner, Rozina spent her days, but every evening, the monster asked the same question, which she kept answering in the negative, whereupon the monster always left in a sad mood. After having spent a fortnight in this wonderful world, she became eager to know how her relatives at home were doing. She told the monster so in the evening. He explained to her that, if she wanted to know this, she could see it in the large mirror in her bedroom upstairs. When she went to bed, she looked in the mirror and saw that her father, even though he looked sad, and her sisters were all well—thank God!

After a few days, however, she saw her father (whom she had constantly seen sad in the mirror because of her) now lying sick in bed. He was lying there very lonely. There was only a servant looking after him. Both her elder sisters were not with him. They had not changed for the better; they had little love for their father and were constantly entertaining themselves in the town. When she saw all this, Rozina wept loudly and longed ardently to be able to look after her father for a while.

At seven in the evening, the monster arrived as usual and asked again: "Rozina, will you be my wife?"

Rozina said she would think about it, but told him about what she had seen in the mirror that morning.

The monster said, "Yes, you may nurse your dear father, but you may not stay away more than seven days. By then, your father will be nursed back to health. But if you stay away longer, Rozina, I will die of grief."

She promised him she would strictly comply with all his wishes and went to bed. How surprised she was, when the next morning at her arousal, she noticed that she had slept in her own ordinary room at home. She could hardly believe her eyes and rubbed them thoroughly. The wonderful garments with the gem stones she had been wearing the previous day were lying over a chair in the room. She dressed herself in them and went downstairs. All her relatives were first under the impression of facing a princess and admired the elegant garments, but they could hardly believe this to be Rozina. She embraced her father cordially and also greeted her sisters. They were somewhat more amicable and friendly towards Rozina than usual, especially when she had told everything and it became clear that she could only stay for seven days. Then she gave the most precious jewels on her dress to her sisters; they both admired the beautiful gifts and were delighted with them. As a result of this, Rozina now had a more agreeable life at home than ever before. Her beloved father's condition improved remarkably, which he contributed to Rozina's presence. The week flew by; full of sadness, they were all thinking of her departure the final morning. Her father, who had a hard time being separated from his daughter again so soon, begged her to stay just a few days longer—surely, the good monster would hardly notice. Rozina yielded to the temptation and agreed.

She had already stayed the eighth day, when she dreamt about the magic palace that night. She heard crying for help, combined with awful moaning. She went to the flower garden the sound came from and saw the poor monster lying on the ground, dying, struck by an arrow through the heart. This was such a terrible shock to the girl that it woke her up.

She got dressed and told the dream to her father, who said, "Rozina, I also believe it is true; you must go and rescue the poor monster."

They embraced each other cordially and Rozina set out for the forest. Again, she suddenly stood in front of the magic palace. Immediately she rushed to the garden and saw the good monster lying there, on his deathbed indeed; she did not see an arrow, but there was a gaping wound near the heart, from which the blood was flowing.

As he was dying, the monster spoke, "Rozina, see . . . this wound . . . you have given me . . . by your . . . disobedience . . . and ingratitude . . . and now . . . must I die . . . farewell sweet Rozina . . . ."

Suffering from convulsions, the monster turned over. The agony of death had set in . . . .

Rozina could not bear to watch any longer. She burst into tears, begged the monster's forgiveness for her disobedience, and full of pity and despair, she exclaimed, "I do not want you to die through my fault; please tell me how I could still help you. I will do anything for you; you have been so good to me."

The monster looked at her appealingly and hopefully, then said: "The only means to save me would be for you to marry me."

Rozina then said, "If this is the only means for me to save you and show my gratitude, I heartily wish to marry you."

And behold . . . ! Hardly had she spoken these words, than the dying monster disappeared, and in his place appeared in front of her a beautiful, slender prince, dressed in splendid silk and damask clothes, bordered with ermine, sparkling with diamonds and precious stones; on his head he was wearing a precious hat studded with jewels, with beautiful feathers hanging down from it.

In admiration, Rozina had taken some steps back, but the prince amiably took her by the hand and said, "Dear Rozina, I thank you a thousand times for saving me from death. Once upon a time a wicked fairy changed me into a monster. And I could only return to my human shape if there would be a woman who would be prepared to marry me as a monster. Then the fairy disappeared. You will be able to imagine what a sad life I was leading and I thought that no woman would ever want to marry me in such guise. Until you, sweet Rozina, consented to it."

Rozina now was very pleased with what had happened and loved the good prince passionately. She then went to collect her father and both her sisters and told them everything. But hardly had they all returned to the castle when they witnessed the appearance of the wicked fairy, who now changed both the vain daughters Louise and Irma into two marble pillars supporting the front gallery. By way of punishment, they had to remain standing like this forever. The wicked fairy became reconciled with the prince and the entire family. Afterwards they celebrated a splendid wedding, which lasted three days. There was a great ball, which was very magnificent, accompanied by wonderful music. This feast was attended by the father, and the prince with his bride Rozina, who was so radiant with splendour and beauty that she could be called the queen of the ball. The attending guests were the wicked fairy and many beautiful goddesses and fairies and all the noblemen and princes of the land. Everyone's beautiful, magnificent costumes were almost dazzling. Noone remembered ever having celebrated such a splendid wedding. The prince and his beautiful wife, with his father-in-law, lived happily and contentedly and loved each other ardently, in permanent prosperity and peace in the magic palace.

This tale is a version of ATU 425C, *Beauty and the Beast.* The story was sent to collector G. J. Boekenoogen on June 20, 1892, by Mrs. M. R. van der Veer from Driebergen (province of Utrecht). The translation is based on T. Meder, *De magische vlucht* (Amsterdam, 2000), pp. 54–65.

ROSE-RED AND LILY-WHITE

*M*any centuries ago, a forester and his wife lived in a large forest with two beautiful daughters. The elder of the two, aged ten, was called Rose-Red, because of her fresh red complexion and healthy figure. In contrast to her sister, the younger was of slight build and had a fine, transparent white complexion. She was therefore called Lily-White. She was six years of age. They were both sweet girls, whose parents enjoyed them a lot. Rose-Red already helped her mother diligently with her work.

Winter came to an end, but it was still very bleak and cold outdoors. When they had had their dinner in the evening, they gathered comfortably around the hot fireplace. The father then lit his pipe, the mother mended clothes, Rose-Red knitted stockings, and Lily-White played with her doll or worked on sewing a rag doll.

One stormy evening, when the rain was beating heavily against the windows and the entire family was gathered comfortably around the fireplace as usual, there were a few loud knocks on the front door. The knocking gave the children a considerable fright, and the whole company was curious to know who this late guest could be. Mother ordered Rose-Red to open the door and not to be scared. The girl obliged. But how frightened she was when the moonlight did not reveal a traveller, but a large brown bear. She was even more amazed when it began to speak.

"My dear child," it said, "fear me not. I will do you no harm. All I ask is a place to stay for tonight."

Rose-Red went back in and told her parents. Bruin was shown in and given a chair near the fireplace. The mother fetched some food and put fresh straw next to the fireplace for the bear to sleep on. The children had a lot of fun with Bruin and caressed him and stroked his shaggy fur.

When Bruin had finished his meal and sat by the fire again, he told the family who he was. "I live in a large den in the forest. In a large mountain nearby, there live fifty evil dwarfs. Their leader is my worst enemy, who never leaves me in peace. Every day when I set out to look for food, he keeps pursuing me and torments me in all sorts of ways. Whenever I want to catch him, he is too quick for me and rapidly climbs up a tree to get away from me. This evening, I was once more out looking for food. The enemy pursued me again with a large stick he used to threaten me, and for that reason, I ran this way. For fear of him, I lack the courage to return to the den tonight."

They had all listened to the story with great compassion, and the forester decided to go out with several other people the following day to kill the dwarfs. The next day after breakfast—after having thanked Bruin cordially—they opened the front door and heard some nasty moaning, which came from the forest close by. They all followed the sounds and the forester took an axe with him. Having arrived at the place the moaning had come from, they saw an ugly dwarf whose long white beard had got stuck under a big tree, which had been blown down by the storm. Bruin recognized his worst enemy in the dwarf.

The dwarf also recognized the bear, but nevertheless, his agony made him call for help. "Please try to lift the trunk, but do not cut off my beard, because then I will have lost my magic powers."

But the forester, delighted to be able to punish the ugly creature, cut the beard off after all. This enraged the dwarf so much that he wanted to attack the man. The forester, however, boldly took up his axe and used it to smash the dwarf's head in. Then he went back home to fetch some limestone to brick up the only entrance to the mountain, which still contained the other dwarfs. All these evil creatures were now buried alive. Barely had the forester finished this job, when behold!: a handsome prince, dressed in wonderful, magnificent garments, appeared before their eyes.

Before they had a chance to speak, the prince said, "I was the bear you just saw. I want to thank you cordially for your kind reception and for the great service you have done me by killing the dwarfs. At one point, this evil dwarf had transformed me into a bear and driven me out of my castle. He had then taken me to a large den here in the forest, in which I was forced to live from then on and where I had to look for my food like an animal. No sooner would I regain my human shape before he, the dwarf himself, would be dead. This now has happened. As a reward, all four of you will have to come and live in my castle and stay there forever."

The family had all listened to the story attentively and were very glad now that the evil dwarfs had been killed. They sold their house and garden and went to live in the prince's castle. After several years, the prince asked for Rose-Red's hand in marriage, whereupon a large wedding took place. Several years later, Lily-White married one of the prince's brothers, who also was a prince and lived nearby in a splendid castle. Again, they celebrated a large wedding and there was joy all over again. From then on, they all lived peacefully and contentedly, and neither princes nor commoners needed to fear the evil dwarfs ever again, because they had all, without exception, been destroyed.

This tale is a version of ATU 426, *The Two Girls, the Bear and the Dwarf.* The story was sent to collector G. J. Boekenoogen on June 20, 1892, by Mrs. M. R. van der Veer from Driebergen (province of Utrecht). The translation is based on T. Meder, *De magische vlucht* (Amsterdam, 2000), pp. 66–68.

THE FROG

A poor woman lived in the country with her three daughters. On a certain feast day, she would make pancakes. The eldest daughter was sent out to draw water from the well. When she pulled up the bucket, there was a frog in it.

"Frog, would you get out of there?" she asked.

Its reply was, "If you are willing to marry me."

"Not on your life!" said the girl. She emptied the bucket and drew again, but no matter how often she tried, the frog was back in the water every time. Eventually, she came home empty handed.

Then the second daughter went out, but returned with the same result.

Finally, the youngest daughter ventured the journey, and when she too was made the demand of a marriage, she consented to it. Immediately, the frog leapt from the bucket. The girl drew clean water and went home, whilst her fiancé was tripping along behind her.

Now the mother started making pancakes. Everybody was enjoying them, and the frog, sitting next to the chair of his bride, was given his share so generously that he constantly tumbled down when he tried to climb the stairs, because he had become so fat and round from all this food. In the end, the girl picked him up and carried him to the small spare room, where he would be spending the night.

When dawn broke, she heard more hustle and bustle from this room than was to be expected from such a tiny animal, and when the door opened, a handsomely dressed prince appeared. He told her he had been bewitched and transformed into a frog. Only the promise of marriage to a sweet girl could save him. And her reward was, of course, that she would now become a princess, while the other sisters would perish with envy and remorse.

This tale is a version of ATU 440, *The Frog King or Iron Henry*. The story was sent to collector G. J. Boekenoogen on February 3, 1894, by A. M. van Cappelle from Arnhem (province of Gelderland). The translation is based on T. Meder, *De magische vlucht* (Amsterdam, 2000), pp. 75–76.

THE LITTLE MAGIC FISH

An old fairy tale retold in rhymes

In a landscape full of dunes,
And not so distant from the sea,
There once lived a dwarfish couple,
By the name of "Piggelmee."

They were tiny little people
And they lived—'twas all they got,
Because they didn't own a house—
In an ancient Cologne pot.

As a shelter for the sunshine,
Or when rain should come to land,
They had put this earthen pot
Upside down into the sand.

A little hole, that was their door,
They'd cast it in with all their might,
So that their little dwarfish bodies
Could easily crawl inside.

The woman, she prepared the food,
At least, if there was any there.
The little man went out to hunt,
To shoot a rabbit or a hare.

He had a tiny little rifle,
With which he shot, this little gnome,
And as soon as he shot his rabbit,
His wooden shoes took him straight home.

Though their housing wasn't rich,
They still enjoyed their life a lot,
And lived for many happy years,
In their topsy-turvy pot.

Who could guess what happened next?
Tidings of the unexpected,
Always come along your door,
When you least expect it.

One lovely summer morning,
In the Dwarf's Gazette, for sure,
They read a magic little fish,
Had arrived upon their shore.

The magic fish swam up and down
The salty waves and sandy bay;
He can give you all you wish for,
If you ask him in a humble way.

That morning, in the old pot,
It became very quiet indeed,
As both dwarfs sadly thought,
How much they were in need.

Asking humbly . . . get it all . . .
Everything, and just be meek.
A little fish that could work magic . . .
Magic? . . . "My husband, did you speak?"

"Who? Me? No!"—"Would you
Dare to go visit the fish?"
"My dearest wife, I would.
I will go and make a wish."

"And . . . what would you wish for,
If you met the fish for sure?"
"I would ask him for a little house,
With a chimney, roof and door."

"Just imagine: a real cottage.
Dare you ask him, my brave spouse?
Real estate with a real door . . . oh!
Dare you ask him for a house?"

"Me living in a house, I say.
Who would have thought, oh boy!"
She said as in a dream,
While her eyes glistened with joy.

The next morning, very early,
There he went, brave Piggelmee,
Clumping in his wooden shoes,
Through the dunes towards the sea.

"Magic fish!" he called from far,
And his voice was loud and clear.
"Fish, I'd like to talk to you;
Oh, are you somewhere near?"

Suddenly, he heard an answer,
From the wide and open sea.
A soft and silvery voice replied,
"Did you call me, Piggelmee?"

"I did, I did," the small dwarf shouted,
While jumping up and down a lot.
"Please, magic fish, give me a house,
Instead of an ancient Cologne pot."

"Go home, go home!" the fish called out:
"I grant your wish with all due care.
Run home in haste, my dwarfish friend,
Because your dwelling is already there."

Without a thanks, the dwarf returned,
Which wasn't very kind;
And instead a piece of earthenware,
A cosy cottage did he find.

Out of a window, the woman waved.
She was as happy as could be.
"Piggelmee! Who would have thought?
A lovely house for you and me!"

Piggelmee was flabbergasted.
This was a house fit for a gnome!
Just like a well-raised gentleman
He wanted to enter his home.

But instead his wife came out.
"This house is nice and all," she said,
"But still you would be disappointed,
For many things are lacking yet."

"Please return to the sea once more,
And call the fish with all your might,
Because what good is such a cottage
With no furniture inside?"

"Ask the fish for seats and sofas,
A clock, a table and a bed,
Ask for curtains in the windows
And a kitchen sink," she said.

"There is more, so walk along now;
I need more things, I'm telling you.
I need a mirror and a sideboard,
And I need a cupboard too."

With a cheerful whistle he went back,
Our little dwarf called Piggelmee.
He walked to the beach and called from far,
"Can you hear me, magic fish in the sea?"

There was no answer, nothing moved,
In the sea nor in the air,
Except for a lonely albatross,
Who did not listen, did not care.

Finally, there was that voice again,
Soft and silvery from the open sea.
"Did you call me again, my little man?
Did you call me, little Piggelmee?"

"Yes, I did!" the dwarf said, pleased.
"I thank you for the wish you granted,
But there is more, like chairs and a bed,
And other furniture we wanted."

"Go home, go home!" the fish called out:
"I grant your wish with all due care.
Run home in haste, my dwarfish friend,
Your furniture is already there."

The Little Magic Fish

Returning home, our little dwarf saw,
His wife working like never before.
While she polished the furniture,
She gave him some orders once more.

"Husband, please, go back again,
So the fish can make me really glad.
Let him give me proper clothes,
And some mantles and a hat."

"Ask for yourself some decent shoes,
Because—and this is commonly known—
You can't walk around in wooden shoes
In a tidy cottage like our own."

Although he started to get tired now,
He turned around, dwarf Piggelmee,
And clumping in his wooden shoes,
Went back to the fish in the sea.

He did not mind to cross the dunes,
But now it started to get dull.
Right above him flew the albatross,
Who got company from a gull.

"Magic fish!" he called from far,
"It's not really my idea, you see,
To return and ask for more,
But my wife is forcing me."

"See, she wants to have more clothes,
And some mantles and a hat,
And a decent pair of shoes for me;
The fish, she said, can give us that."

"All right!" the magic fish replied,
"I know how women have their way;
Now go on home as fast you can,
To see that everything's okay."

When the dwarf arrived at home,
His wife looked, fully dressed,
In admiration in the mirror.
"I am so sorry now," she stressed,

"But you'll have to go back again.
I can't go out, I am afraid,
Without someone taking care of things.
Piggelmee, we need a maid!"

"Go and tell the magic fish,
That I can't cope here on my own;
Or do I have to cook and bake,
And scrub here all alone?"

For the first time now, the little dwarf
Looked at his wife in sheer dismay,
But still—oh well—went on his way;
He did not dare a thing to say.

On his way he kept on thinking
How happy they had been before.
And now . . . they were most fortunate,
But . . . he didn't whistle anymore.

"Magic fish," he called from far,
"Magic fish here in the sea!"
"Are you calling again?" the fish asked,
"Are you calling, Piggelmee?"

"I am. My wife would like some help,"
Said Piggelmee, a bit afraid.
"She wants some help around the house;
That's why I'm asking for a maid."

Since the fish kept silent for a while,
The dwarf feared he was gone,
But then a voice came from the sea,
"I expected so, my little one."

"Go home, and you will find
That everything is neat and clean,
Thanks to a maid, a little dwarf,
As tidy as you've never seen."

Piggelmee, though tired of walking,
Longed for home, so home he went.
Halfway home he met his wife,
Who looked at him in discontent.

"You need to go back this instant,
Because the situation just got worse:
I went shopping, only to discover
There's not a penny in my purse."

"Go ask the fish another favour,
A bag of money is what I need.
I have to pay the maid, don't I ?
After this, you may rest your feet."

To visit the magic fish once more,
The dwarf returned with leaden pace.
Meanwhile, it was getting late;
The beach became a desolate place.

A sneaking weasel startled him.
All animals—to him—looked tall,
Not because they were so big,
But because he was so small.

"Magic fish," he called from far,
"Magic fish here in the sea!"
"You called?" a cheerful voice replied,
"You called, friend Piggelmee?"

"I did!" replied the dwarf relieved:
"Yes, my wife sends me once more;
She has to pay the maid, you see,
And wants to buy things in a store."

"As far as our house is concerned
We've got everything we need,
But according to my dearest wife,
It's money we lack, indeed."

"Go home!" the fish suddenly said.
"I grant your wish with all due care.
I should have known you needed money.
Now go home, it is already there."

Now the fish vanished into the deep.
The dwarf went home, the sun went down.
His wife counted the money from the bag,
While sitting in her dressing gown.

The next day, it was very cosy
In the dwelling of the gnome.
Piggelmee, who used to hunt all day,
Instead now drank his coffee home.

"This coffee doesn't taste so good;
We drank this when we were poor.
Now that we are rich," said Piggelmee,
"We need not drink this anymore."

"The maid tried to buy a better brand,
But she did not succeed.
Perhaps you could ask the magic fish
What kind of coffee we do need."

"That's a good idea," the dwarf replied.
On his leather shoes, as proud as can be,
Piggelmee strolled towards the shore
Where he called the magic fish in the sea.

"I'm not here to beg, just for your advice.
Which coffee is better than the rest?"
A silvery snout surfaced from the water
and said: "Van Nelle* coffee is the best."

The maid bought the coffee and indeed,
There was no better; the fish was right.
The dwarves could not think of a better life.
And seemed forever satisfied.

Alas, nothing seems to last forever,
Not even satisfaction, that's for sure.
People always wish for something new;
They long for better, best, and more.

Now . . . several months have passed,
And we see our friend Piggelmee
Strolling on a daily basis,
To the magic fish in the sea.

He was always sent out by his wife;
There was always something to complain.
Slowly her dissatisfaction
Drove our little dwarf insane.

Then the bread did not taste right,
Then the milk had turned bad . . . .
She always sent him out for advice,
And . . . the fish did not even get mad.

One cold morning, he had to go again
To the magic fish in the sea,
To ask him if he knew better coffee
Than Van Nelle, poor Piggelmee.

"I really did not want to come,
I'd rather stayed in bed,
But my wife wants better coffee
Than Van Nelle, now, don't get mad."

The waves turned black, the water boiled.
"Here's a message your wife can't miss,"
The magic fish replied in anger.
"Van Nelle is the best there is!

I'm sorry for you, but I punish your wife
For being discontented and greedy.
Go back now and behold your new state.
You'll again be poor and needy."

The magic fish vanished into the water,
The sea turned calm and blue once more.
Piggelmee was afraid to go home,
But as the sun set, he left the shore.

Like a beaten dog he walked back home,
Slowly he felt his limbs grow weak.
A partridge flew into the sky
With a horrifying shriek.

Slower and slower he walked.
Each shoe seemed to weigh a ton,
More than his wooden shoes ever weighed,
In the good old days bygone.

Once home, he looked around
Disappointed—and so he should!—
For the ancient Cologne pot returned
Where once the cosy cottage stood.

His wife sat outside and cried,
"It is ill fate, oh Piggelmee,
That we now have to live again
In this old pot—don't you agree?"

"Oh, and I would not complain
As long as I have you, my sweet,
And a few cups of coffee a day.
This is such a cruel defeat."

After a night of little sleep,
Shaking for cold and deep remorse,
Piggelmee visited the fish again,
To ask for one last thing, of course.

"Magic fish," Piggelmee called out:
"Would you please hear my apology?
Would you come to the surface
And, for one more time, listen to me?"

"My wife is conscious of her guilt;
Her wishes were not very wise.
She is sitting in the ancient pot now
And she is crying out her eyes."

"One thing could console her though,
One small gift could make her dance:
A package of Van Nelle coffee.
Would you give her that last chance?"

"Dear fellow," spoke the magic fish.
"All I do, I do for you.
I care not for your wife: she's greedy,
And she is ungrateful, too."

"I wish to grant you a little comfort;
That is because for you I care.
So go on home, my dearest dwarf,
For your coffee is already there."

As he approached his ancient house,
He already smelled that familiar scent
Of fresh coffee that made Piggelmee
And his wife feel most content.

The dwarfs accepted their fate,
Soon filling the room with laughter,
While drinking little cups of coffee,
And living happily ever after.

---

*Brand name of a famous Dutch coffee (and tobacco) company.

This is a commercial version of the well-known fairy tale ATU 555, *The Fisher and His Wife*. This Dutch version was made into a book in 1920 by L. G. Steenhuisen, senior sales representative of the Van Nelle coffee company. In order to obtain the pictures that needed to be glued into the book, people had to buy the coffee. Since the book was such a success, Piggelmee more or less became the standard name for the dwarf in the story, while the pictures gave many people a distinct image of what the dwarf looked like. My translation in rhymes of Steenhuisen's *Van het tovervisje. Een oud sprookje opnieuw verteld en berijmd* is based on the photographic reprint made in Rotterdam in 1971. Towards the end of the story the commercial message became a bit too elaborate for my taste, so I took the liberty of abbreviating the text here and there. Of course, in the real folktale, the coffee brand plays no role at all. The female dwarf turns all greedy and wishes for the impossible, for instance, to become queen or even God. Then she and her husband are punished by the magic fish, and they end up in poverty in their Cologne pot (or chamber pot in some oral versions of the story) again. Most of the time, the lesson to be learned from the story is to be satisfied with what you have.

The Little Magic Fish   **53**

A PRODIGY

*O*nce upon a time there was a queen, and this queen desperately wanted to have a child. Every morning that God gave, she went to an isolated part of the garden to pray for a child, but to no avail.

Suddenly one morning, as she was praying again, an angel descended from heaven and said to her, "You can set your mind at ease. Your prayer will be answered. Soon you will receive a child—and this child shall be a prodigy, for all his wishes will come true."

In a state of bliss, the queen went to the king; she told him what had just happened to her, and the king—what else would you expect?—was delighted as can be.

After a while, the queen gave birth to a son, and the boy was as beautiful as can be.

Every morning the queen took the little boy for a walk in the garden. He grew and grew and developed a healthy color in his cheeks. All the nobility at the king's court enjoyed the boy's presence, and they loved and adored him, because he was such a sweet boy.

Now, what you need to know is, that there was a cook at the king's court, and he was a bad person. On many occasions, he had already thought, "If the boy would be mine, I could profit from his miraculous powers."

On a hot sizzling day, the queen fell asleep on a bench in the garden. Secretly, the cook took the boy away and smeared some blood on the queen's sleeve. He brought the boy to a cabin in the woods to have him raised there. He went back to the king and told him that the queen did not take care of her son well enough and that some wild animal had devoured him.

As you can imagine, the king was very angry. He had the queen thrown into a dark dungeon, had her sealed up alive, so that she would die of hunger. However, our sweet Lord, knowing that she was innocent, took care of her, and every day He sent her two white doves from heaven (angels they were), who brought her food and drink.

After waiting for seven years, the cook finally thought that it was about time to benefit from the wonder boy.

He resigned from the king's service, went to the cabin where the boy was concealed, and said, "My boy, now wish yourself a lovely large castle, with a beautiful garden with flowers and a fruit-tree and a pond and a summer house and all kinds of other beautiful things."

And lo and behold, as the angel had predicted, the little boy's wish came true: a castle, a garden with flowers and a fruit-tree, and a pond and summer house and all.

After they had lived there for a while, the cook said, "Now wish yourself a companion to play with—a girl as pretty as you can imagine."

The words had barely left his mouth, when there stood a girl so pretty that no painter would be able to portray her more beautifully.

Every day the children played with each other, and more and more they started to fall in love with one another. Meanwhile, the cook lived like a lord in his castle: a stiff drink in the morning, a hunting party in the afternoon, and in the evening the spirit bottle was put on the table once more. Still, he began to get a little worried. He kept fearing that the boy, whose intellect increased by the day, would wish to see his father and his mother, and he realized that could turn out badly for him.

So one day he said to the prince's girlfriend, "As soon as he is asleep, go to his bed quietly and push this knife into his heart. If you refuse, it will be time for you to die. As proof that you have done what I have ordered you, you need to bring me his heart and his tongue."

The girl, however, didn't want to do this. She loved the prince very much and she thought, I won't take orders from you!

She had a young goat slaughtered that had recently been born in the stable, and she brought the goat's heart and tongue to the cook. She told the prince about the cook, and told him to hide.

The cook suspected that he was being deceived. He went looking for the prince, and found him in his bed, hiding under the sheets.

Immediately, the young prince jumped up and shouted, "I wish that you turn into a black poodle, and that the only thing you eat will be red-hot charcoal, so that the flames will leak out of your mouth—and to enable me to recognize you all the time, you will wear a golden chain around your neck."

These words were barely spoken, when the cook changed into a black poodle. The girl called a servant to bring the dog a pot of red-hot charcoal and, indeed, the flames leaked from his mouth.

After that, the young prince started longing for his mother terribly, and no one was able to talk him out of this desire, so one day he said to his companion, "I am returning to my country, and you can come along if you like."

The girl couldn't face the long journey, so to make it easy for her, the prince wished that she would change into a flower. Of course, the wish came true. He put the flower into his buttonhole, grabbed his staff, and took off on his journey, with the black poodle walking right behind him.

After a long trip and several adventures, the prince finally arrived at the dungeon where his mother was held captive.

Through the prison window he called her, "My dear sweet mother, honorable queen, are you still alive?"

His mother, however, thought that this came from the doves that brought her food and drink every day, and she said, "I have food enough, sweet angels."

"That's not what I'm talking about," said the prince: "I am your son, who is supposed to have been eaten by a wild animal, but that was a lie. I am still alive and I've returned."

Next, the prince went to the king and asked him if he were in need of a hunter.

"Yes, I am," the king said, "but there is very little game in the woods right now."

"No problem," said the prince, "I can catch them anyhow."

"That I would like to see," the king said, and he called for his men, and they went on a hunting party together.

As soon as they entered the forest, the prince wished for all kinds of game, and the hare, rabbits, deer. and wild boars came running from all sides, and within half an hour they had a high cart full of game.

The king ordered his servants to organize a large banquet, since he had not had so much game in the cellar for a long time. He told the new hunter to sit in the honorary seat to his right.

As they were all eating, the prince wished that one of the noblemen would bring up his mother. He had hardly wished it, when the Lord Chamberlain arose and said, "Your Majesty, now that we are having such a good time and there is plenty of everything, I just wondered what became of the queen. Is she still alive, or did she die from hunger a long time ago?"

The king got angry and said, "Don't speak to me about the queen. She let a wild animal eat my only son."

At that moment, the new hunter stood up and said, "Father, I am your son, and my mother is still alive. The wild animals haven't eaten me. The cook, that old scoundrel, took me away and smeared blood on my mother's sleeve, so that you would believe his story. Here's the scoundrel," he said, and dragging the black poodle with his chain collar before the king, he ordered for a pot of red-hot charcoal, which the dog ate while the flames leaped from his mouth.

Next, the king requested to behold the rascal as he had known him before, and the prince had barely finished his wish, when there the cook stood with his white apron on, his white chef's hat on his head and a large knife in his hand.

The king recognized him at once, and ordered his guards to seize him and lock him in the prison tower.

Then the prince said to the king, "Father, now I want you to meet the girl who always cheered me up during my exile and who spared my life when the cook wanted to kill me."

"With pleasure," the king said.

The prince took the flower from his buttonhole and showed it to the king. The king said that he had never seen such a beautiful flower, but then the prince made his wish, and the flower changed into a pretty young woman. No one in the whole kingdom had ever seen such a beautiful girl.

Now the king sent his chamberlains to the queen to release her from the dungeon and to bring her back to the castle. However, the queen refused to participate in the banquet. Indeed, she didn't want anything to drink or eat anymore.

"Our Sweet Lord in heaven," she said, "did not forsake me when I was locked into the dungeon innocently. I suppose He will come and get me very soon now."

So it happened. Three days later, she died. When she was taken to the churchyard with much wealth and splendor, two white doves flew over her coffin. These were the angels that had always brought her food and drink.

The king had the crooked cook cut to pieces with a butcher's knife, but after that, he started mourning; his heart was broken, and quite soon they had to carry him to the churchyard as well.

So it was that the prince became king. He married the beautiful girl, and she became queen. For many, many years they have ruled the country. And if they aren't dead, they are still alive.*

---

*This is one of the traditional formulas to end a fairy tale in Dutch: "En als ze niet dood zijn, dan leven ze nog." Another formula is, "Then there came an elephant with a long trunk, and he blew the whole story to an end." ("Toen kwam er een olifant met een lange snuit en die blies het hele verhaaltje uit.")

This fairy tale is the only version of ATU 652, *The prince whose wishes always come true,* that has ever been collected in the Netherlands. It was taken down by collector August Hendrik Sassen (1853–1913), probably around 1890, in the neighbourhood of Helmond (North Brabant). The translation from dialect is based on Willem de Blécourt, *Volksverhalen uit Noord-Brabant* (Utrecht and Antwerp, 1980), pp. 96–99.

THE EVIL STEPMOTHER

*F*ather had given Jan and Betje a stepmother. It did not take long for the children to notice that she was an evil woman. She spoke unfriendly to father, grumbled to Betje, and beat little Jantje.* She even locked him up in the attic and scared him so much that he tried to avoid her as often as possible. One day the stepmother bought a basket of apples. Jantje was very fond of apples, but just to torment him, the stepmother gave only Betje an apple every once in a while, and told her that she had to eat it right away, so that she couldn't share it with Jan.

One Friday when father and Betje were not home, the stepmother said to Jan, "Would you like a beautiful red apple?"

"Yes please, mother," Jan replied in astonishment.

"Then go to the attic and take one; you can find them in the big chest."

Jan went up, but soon he called, "Mother, I'm unable to open the chest."

"Wait," she said, "I will help you."

She opened the heavy lid of the chest. As Jan bent over to get himself an apple, she let the heavy lid fall down and little Jantje was killed instantly. His head lay inside the chest with the apples, his body outside. Then the mother took the body, cut it into little pieces, and threw all the flesh in a kettle of boiling soup.

When father and Betje came home, she called to them, "I've made some delicious soup; come quick and eat!"

"Where is Jan?" father asked, "or is he being punished again?"

"He is in his hide, if he isn't skinned," was the coarse answer.

After they had finished supper, Betje had to throw away the bones. She put them under the lime tree and took the opportunity to look up to the attic window, because she suspected that Jan would be sitting over there, but she couldn't see a thing. Meanwhile, father and Betje became worried, because Jantje had not returned home.

The next day, a little bird flew from the lime tree and came to sit on the windowsill.

The bird sang:

> *"Riktiktik,** here I am,*
> *Riktiktik, here I am."*

"It's Jantje's voice," father and Betje both said, and they went to the window. Then the small bird flew to the chimney and sang with a sad little voice:

> *"My mother slew me,*
> *My father ate me.*
> *My sister buried my bones under the lime tree,*
> *And rikketikketik, here I am."*

Then the same voice called,

> *"Father, father, come here."*
> *"Jan, Jan, what must I do?"*
> *"Father, father, come here."*
> *"Jan, Jan, what must I do?"*
> *"Father, father, come here."*
> *"Jan, Jan, what must I do?"*

Then the father stood under the chimney and a new hat fell on his head.

The next Friday, the little bird flew out of the tree once more, went to sit on the windowsill again, then flew to the chimney, and sang:

> *"My mother slew me,*
> *My father ate me.*
> *My sister threw my bones under the lime tree,*
> *And rikketikketik, here I am."*

Then he called,

> *"Betje, Betje, come here."*
> *"Jan, Jan, what must I do?"*
> *"Betje, Betje, come here."*
> *"Jan, Jan, what must I do?"*
> *"Betje, Betje, come here."*
> *"Jan, Jan, what must I do?"*

Then Betje stood under the chimney and a golden brooch fell on her head.

You see, the next Friday the bird returned again. First he pecked against the window, flew to the chimney afterwards, and sang once more:

> *"My mother slew me,*
> *My father ate me.*
> *My sister threw my bones under the lime tree,*
> *And rikketikketik, here I am."*

The Evil Stepmother

Again he called,

"Mother, mother, come here."
"Jan, Jan, what must I do?"
"Mother, mother, come here."
"Jan, Jan, what must I do?"
"Mother, mother, come here."
"Jan, Jan, what must I do?"

The stepmother then stepped under the chimney, expecting something beautiful as well, but instead there fell a millstone on her head, and she was as dead as a doornail.

---

*Actually, the *-tje* in Jantje already means "little."

**This mimics the sound of light tapping on the window.

This tale is a version of ATU 720, *The Juniper Tree.* In the nineteenth and twentieth centuries it was found many times in the oral tradition of the Netherlands. This particular story was sent to collector G. J. Boekenoogen in June 1892 by the sisters Roorda from Assen (province of Drente). The translation is based on T. Meder, *De magische vlucht* (Amsterdam, 2000), pp. 90–93.

THE ROSE VIOLET

*O*nce upon a time there were a father and a mother, who had two children. One was called Jantje, the other was called Mietje.

One day the father decided to go out of town. The father then said to Jantje, "I'm going out of town. What would you like me to bring along for you as a welcome gift?"

Jantje then said, "Father, keep your money, save your money and use it to buy bread and biscuits."

But the father said, "No, I want you to have something anyway."

"Well," said Jantje, "make it a gold watch then."

Then the father said to Mietje, "Mietje, I'm going out of town. What would you like to have as a welcome gift?"

Mietje then said, "Keep your money, save your money and use it to buy bread and biscuits."

"No," said the father, "I want you to have something anyway."

"Well," said Mietje, "make it a rose violet then."

The father went on his journey, and bought the presents, although it was a lot of trouble to purchase the rose violet. Jantje and Mietje were very pleased with their gifts. Shortly afterwards, Mietje and Jantje went for a walk, Janje with his watch and Mietje with her rose violet.

Jantje then said to Mietje, "How about swapping the rose violet for the gold watch?"

"No," said Mietje.

Then Jantje got angry and said, "I will ask you three more times, and if you don't want to oblige me, then I will kill you. The rose violet for me and the gold watch for you?"

"No."

"The rose violet for me and the gold watch for you?"

"No."

"The rose violet for me and the gold watch for you?"

"No."

Then Jantje grabbed hold of his sister, beat her to death, and buried her in the sand.

When Jantje arrived home, his father asked, "Jantje, how come your shirt is covered in blood?"

"I've been to the butcher's, watching the slaughter," Jantje said, "and then the blood splattered all over my shirt."

The father appeared to be satisfied with this answer. Not a word was said about Mietje, and it appeared that she was not even missed! For the story continues like this: Several days later, Jantje goes for a walk with his father and mother and the maid. By a mere chance, they are walking past the place where Jantje buried Mietje. And behold, on the grave is growing a rose violet.

The father sees this and says, "Look here! It has taken me so much trouble to buy a rose violet, and look, it's growing so close to home!"

The father—and now it becomes all the more apparent that Mietje is still not missed—wants to pick the rose violet to give it to Mietje when he comes home. But as soon as he touches the rose, there is a voice from the grave, saying,

> *"Oh father dear, oh father dear,*
> *Let me keep this rose, by God*
> *For Jantje killed me here, for shame.*
> *I lie here smothered in my blood."*

Then the father says to mother, "Just you pick this flower."

When the mother touches it, there is a voice from the grave, saying,

> *"Oh mother dear, oh mother dear,*
> *Let me keep this rose, by God*
> *For Jantje killed me here, for shame.*
> *I lie here smothered in my blood."*

Then the father says to the maid that she has to pick the flower, but also when she touches it, the voice says,

> *"Oh Kaatje dear, oh Kaatje dear,*
> *Let me keep this rose, by God*
> *For Jantje killed me here, for shame.*
> *I lie here smothered in my blood."*

Then Jantje is told to pick it, but then the voice speaks, with a horrifying sound:

> *"Oh murderer, oh murderer,*
> *Let me keep this rose, by God*
> *For you, you killed me here, for shame.*
> *I lie here smothered in my blood,*
> *Let me now keep this rose, by God."*

Now it becomes apparent that Jantje had killed Mietje. The father is furious with Jantje and lets him choose his death: either he could be drawn and quartered, or he could jump from a tall building. Jantje chooses the latter thing and dies a horrible death.

This tale is a version of ATU 780, *The Singing Bone*, and was sent to collector G. J. Boekenoogen on January 19, 1892, by Mrs. J. Mandings from Alkmaar (province of North Holland). The translation is based on T. Meder, *De magische vlucht* (Amsterdam, 2000), pp. 93–96.

Part 3

RELIGIOUS TALES

SAINT NICOLAS AND THE THREE STUDENTS

*T*hree students of noble descent were on their way to a city where they wanted to attend the university. One evening, on their journey through a desolate area, they found shelter at an inn. The innkeeper, who suspected that the students carried along a lot of golden coins, decided to kill them that very night. After he had carried out his sinister plan, he cut the bodies of the students to pieces, and put the pieces of meat in a barrel of salt, like one does with slaughtered pigs.

Warned by an angel, Saint Nicolas knocked at the door of the inn the next day, asked for accommodation, and ordered a meal. Saint Nicolas was offered a plate of human flesh and immediately confronted the innkeeper with his crime and he ordered the innkeeper to show him the barrel of salt, in which the pieces of the youngsters had been put. Standing near the barrel, Saint Nicolas ordered the innkeeper to take the lid off the barrel. Then he folded his hands, prayed to God, and blessed the three students. That way, he revived them. The three students stepped out of the barrel and thanked God. The innkeeper fell to his knees, asked for forgiveness, and converted to a good Christian life.

This West European legend confirms the patronage of Saint Nicolas over children; in the Netherlands, the feast of Saint Nicolas, who brings gifts for all children, is celebrated annually on the eve of his dying day, December 5. The story was sent by e-mail to the Meertens Instituut on December 5, 2005, by storyteller Rens de Vette from Arnhem (province of Gelderland). The translation is based on this (unpublished) tale (archive and Dutch Folktale Database, Meertens Instituut, Amsterdam).

SAINT BONIFACE

W hen Boniface* arrived in Dokkum with his followers, he was very thirsty. He asked for something to drink, but nobody would give him any water. When his horse scraped the ground with his hoof, suddenly water emerged from the earth. The horse had been able to smell the water. Then they were all able to drink for a while. Livestock is always attracted to water. This all happened at the location where today the Bonifatius fountain can be found.

On another occasion Boniface and his followers came to Dokkum, and they were all very hungry. When Boniface went to the baker for some bread, he refused to give him any. The baker claimed that he did not have any bread.

Then Boniface asked him, "What do you have in the oven then?" He most certainly smelled bread.

The baker answered, "Stones."

Later on, when the baker wanted to take the bread out of the oven, it appeared to be stones. The bread had turned into stone.

---

*Boniface or Bonifatius (672–754) was a British missionary who tried to convert the Frisians to Christianity. He was killed by some Frisians near Dokkum in 754.

These two legends can be catalogued as SINLEG 0416, *Heiliger lässt Brunnen entspringen* (saint makes a well rise) and VDK 0751E*, *De stenen broden* (the stone bread), today also known as ATU 751G*, *Bread Turned to Stone*. The legends were told to collector A. A. Jaarsma on June 2, 1965, by Mrs. Geeske Kobus-Van der Zee from Nijega (Friesland). The tales have not been published so far (Jaarsma Collection, report 385, tales no. 8 and 9; archive and Dutch Folktale Database, Meertens Instituut, Amsterdam).

BLASPHEMY

*O*nce upon a time there was a farmer on the Veluwe,* who lived a godless life, and maintained with a smile on his face, "Nobody can harm a farmer, because a farmer does not have to worry about a thing, and all the other people have to obey the farmer."

Christmas night had come; no snow was on the fields yet, but it was freezing outside, the soil was rigid, black, and solid as a rock, and the farmer said to his wife, "I'm going to gather wood now. The roads are passable everywhere, the sky is clear, the moon is shining and soon a nice fire will be burning, to cook porridge."

"Don't go looking for brushwood or branches in the Christmas night. I can hear the church bells ringing. God will punish you, if you work on a holy day."

"Trust me, woman, God shall not punish me; farmers may do as they please."

He swung a bag over his shoulder and went on his way. After he had gathered enough wood, he returned home, while he was secretly thinking: "Now my wife will be convinced that a farmer can do what he likes, just because a farmer is a farmer."

Suddenly, he noticed that an invisible and inaudible force was lifting him into the air, higher and higher all the time, straight towards the moon, until—wham!—he reached the surface of the moon with his bag of brushwood.

On very clear summer nights one can observe the moon, and with the naked eye, one can see that the farmer is the man-in-the-moon, and if one looks closely enough, one can even see his bag full of brushwood.

---

*Rural area in the eastern part of the Netherlands, mainly in the province of Gelderland, today considered to be the Dutch "Bible belt."

This tale is a version of VDK 777A*, *Het mannetje (vrouwtje) in de maan (zon)* (The little man [woman] in the moon [sun]), today also known as ATU 751E*, *Man in the Moon*. The tale is a religious tale, because the sinner is punished by God. The translation of the story is based on J. Cohen, *Nederlandse Volksverhalen* (Zutphen, 1952), p. 150.

Part 4

REALISTIC TALES

THE TAMING OF THE SHREW

$\mathcal{O}$nce upon a time there was a farmer who was married. He had a decent wife all right, but she was quite bossy. She did her work at home, but in the meantime he had to go out and work on the land, no matter what the weather conditions were.

One day in late autumn it was hailing, snowing, and storming violently, but the farmer still had to go out to his land, half an hour away from home.

Of course, there wasn't a single soul outside . . . well, except for a young horse-dealer who was forced to go out to make a living. There he came along with his horse and wagon, but finally the horse became so exhausted that the man stopped for a while. At this point he heard some distinct sighing.

What can this be? he thought, who can be out here just now?

Then again, he heard someone sighing and he decided to go and have a look. Yes, over there, behind a fence, he saw our farmer standing, shivering with cold.

"Whatever are you doing over there?" he asked.

"Oh," said the farmer, "I've got a decent wife, but she cannot stand me being around."

"Well," the horse-dealer said, "today she will have to. Get on, let me drive you home."

So it happened. After they arrived safe and sound, the horse-dealer/merchant took his time to smoke a pipe. They got into conversation with each other, and the merchant stayed for supper and eventually stayed overnight, because of the bad weather conditions.

Well, I must add that the farmer had a daughter, a darn nice girl. The merchant had difficulty saying good-bye to her. Nevertheless, he had to leave. Because he had had such a pleasant time, he returned to visit the family more than once, and it came to the point that he started courting the farmer's daughter and in the end they agreed to get married. He had barely got into his wedding suit, and the bride was still dressing herself, when he heard his mother-in-law talk to his future wife.

"Girl," she said, "be sure to stay in charge at home, just like me."

The daughter promised to do so.

"That doesn't sound good at all," the merchant thought, but he married her anyway. After being married for a while, they went to visit the in-laws.

Again, the mother-in-law took her daughter apart and asked, "Tell me, are you in charge?"

"Yes," she answered, "pretty much, but not entirely yet."

"Well, take care," said the mother, "and remember: I have always been the boss."

This was all the merchant overheard, but after they had come home again, he distinctly noticed that his wife became bossier by the day.

As soon as her temper started to annoy him, he said, "We should visit your mother again. It's such nice weather and we have not been there for quite a while."

His wife agreed. He harnessed the oldest nag he had to the wagon and took along his oldest dog. Now, the dog might be old, but he could still run faster than the horse.

So the man shouted, "Stay behind us!"

The dog kept running in the lead.

"Stay behind!" he shouted once more. "Can't you hear me, darn it?! If I have to say it once again and you won't obey, then I'll stab you to death on the spot."

The dog kept on running though.

"Stay behind, I said," the man shouted for the third time. "Woman, hold the rein for me."

He got down from the wagon and stabbed his dog to death with his knife.

A while later, the horse started to stumble.

"Keep steady," the man said.

A bit further, the horse stumbled again.

"Steady, I said," the man warned his horse for the second time. "If I need to say it once more, I will stab and kill you as well."

Well, the nag stumbled again, and the man stabbed him until he was dead as a doornail.

There the wagon stood still.

"We have to go on," the man said. "Come on, woman, put the horse-collar on."

"No, I won't," the woman said.

"By Jove," he said. "I am ordering you for the second time now, but don't let me say it a third time."

Trembling from fear, the woman obeyed her husband's command, and off they went to her mother, while he was sitting on the wagon with the horsewhip in his hand. One can imagine that they attracted a great deal of attention. The mother saw this spectacle coming from afar, and all who saw it slapped their knees with laughter.

"Whoever can that be?"

"It is Mrs. so and so."

"No," someone else said, "it is Mrs. so and so."

"It can't be my daughter, that's for sure," said the mother, "because she is the boss."

Alas, as they came closer, she saw that it was her daughter after all.

"What on earth is the matter with you?" she asked.

"Oh mother," the daughter replied, "shut up. He killed the dog and he killed the horse, and if I were disobedient once more, he would have killed me too."

After that the couple led a very happy life . . . .

This very conservative (to say the least) tale about the role of men and women is the only version of the folktale type ATU 901, *Taming of the Shrew*, that has ever been taken down from oral tradition in the Netherlands. The collector was Cornelis Bakker (1863–1933), and the story was told to him on November 7, 1901, by dairy farmer Dirk Schuurman (1839–1908) in the dialect of Broek in Waterland (North Holland). The translation is based on T. Meder, *Vertelcultuur in Waterland* (Amsterdam, 2001), pp. 320–321. See "Who's in Charge?" (part 9) for a contrasting tale.

NO WORRIES

*O*nce upon a time there was a king who went out for a ride, like kings sometimes do. He came to a farm with a sign on the gate, which said, No Worries.

That's odd, the king thought; although I am the most privileged person in the whole country, I have plenty of worries. How can there be someone here who has no worries?

So he made the carriage stop and went up to the farmer's wife.

"So, woman," he said, "how's life treating you?"

"Well enough, sir, and how's that with you?"

"Quite good, thank you. Are you happy out here?"

"Can't complain."

"Do you have any worries?"

"I should think so, sir. I've got a bunch of boys to feed, to clothe and to raise; that's quite a job, you know."

"Funny you should say that," the king replied, "because the sign on the gate says, No Worries."

"Yes, well, I didn't put it there," the farmer's wife replied. "It's the landlord who put it there."

"What's the name of your landlord?"

Then the farmer's wife mentioned the name of one of the servants of the king.

"Come again?" the king said.

She repeated the name, and now the king was sure that the farm belonged to one of his court's servants.

The next day the king summoned the servant.

"Well, mate," the king said, "how are you coming along?"

"Quite alright, sir."

"You own a farm, don't you?"

"Yes, sir."

"So you have no worries?"

"No sir, I can cope very nicely; you pay me a good week's wages, too, and I have saved some money for a rainy day, so why should I worry?"

"Right," said the king, "now let me tell you something. I *do* have worries, and I can't stand that people in my service don't have any worries. So I will fire you right this instant and give you something to worry about."

The servant was shocked and asked if there was no alternative.

Finally, the king decided to keep him, provided he could answer three questions within three days:

1. How many buckets does it take to empty the sea?

2. How long does it take to travel around the world?

3. What am I thinking?

Now the servant was even more depressed. As merry as he used to be, he was that worried now. His head sank lower and lower between his shoulders. At a certain moment, he met one of his comrades, who happened to look a lot like him.

"What's the matter?" said the friend. "You look as if you're at your wit's end."

The servant explained the whole matter and finally said, "Now, wouldn't you be upset?"

"Not at all," the other said. "Hand me over your clothes, and I will solve this matter in a decent way."

The servant agreed.

The third day, the friend went to the king.

"Ah," the king said, "there you are. Tell me, how many buckets does it take to empty the sea?"

"Just one," he answered, "provided your bucket is big enough."

"Clever," the king said. "And how many days does it take to travel around the world?"

"Twenty-four hours," he replied, "as long as you sit on the sun."*

"That's really smart," said the king. "Now, what am I thinking?"

"Well," he said, "you think I am your servant, but in fact I am his mate."

The king started laughing, because the other had outwitted him, and he decided the servant was allowed to stay.

---

*According to folk belief at that time, the sun could still circle around the earth, instead of the other way around.

This story is a version of ATU 922, *The Shepherd Substituting for the Clergyman Answers the King's Questions*. On October 7, 1901, this story was told to collector C. Bakker by dairy farmer Dirk Schuurman in Broek in Waterland (North Holland). The translation is based on T. Meder, *De magische vlucht* (Amsterdam, 2000), pp. 98–100.

No Worries

THE THIEF UNDER THE TABLECLOTH

One day, money had disappeared that a while before had been lying on the table. No strangers had visited the farm, so it had to be an inside job. The farmer wanted to know who did it, but neither wife nor children, maid nor farmhand knew anything about it.

So he went to the schoolteacher, because he was a man of resources. He was an old man with a grey beard, who had read many books and had lots of experience of life.

When the schoolteacher came to the farm, he didn't ask a thing. He just said, "Now, let's all go to the front room."

Over there was a table with a large tablecloth.

"Now we all have to sit on our knees and stick our heads under the table," the schoolteacher said.

So it happened. After a moment of silence, he asked, "Are we all here?"

"Yes," everyone answered.

"The thief too?"

"Yes!" said Sievert. He was the farmhand.

This is a version of the folktale type VDK 926E, *Dief ertoe gebracht zichzelf te verraden* (thief provoked to betray himself), more specifically a variant of the third kind, *Alle hoofden onder de tafel* (all heads under the table). The tale was collected by Klaas ter Laan (1871–1963), probably in the first half of the twentieth century, in the province of Groningen. The translation is based on Eelke de Jong and Hans Sleutelaar, *Sprookjes van de Lage Landen* (Amsterdam, 1996), pp. 172–173.

THE SOLDIER AND THE KING

*O*nce upon a time there was a gentleman who got lost in the woods. It started to get dark, and he was looking for a place to spend the night, but there was not a light in sight. As he was walking along, another man caught up with him; the man looked a bit shabby, but still the gentleman was glad to meet a man who could perhaps give him directions. So he asked him where he was going.

"Well," the other man said, "I have to go to the city where the king lives."

"In that case, let's go together," the gentleman proposed, "because that's where I have to go, too. If you don't mind me asking, what's your business with the king?"

"Oh, I am an ex-soldier," said the man, "and I am going to ask the king for a pension."

"Do you think the king will give it to you?"

"If he doesn't, I will take a stone from my pocket and throw it in his face."

"I wouldn't do that," the gentleman said, "because that could cost you your life."

"I don't care," the soldier said, "because if I don't get a pension, I will die from hunger anyhow. It doesn't matter to me how I die."

Talking like this, they walked along and arrived at an inn.

They went inside and found an old maid, who said, "Good heavens, what are you doing here? Twelve robbers live in this place, and as soon as they find you here, you first have to play cards with them, and then they will murder you."

The gentleman was unpleasantly surprised by her words, but the soldier thought, Oh well, I can only die once.

Anyway, there was no time to leave, even if they wanted to, because the robbers came in, wished everyone a good evening, sat at a table, and ordered something to drink.

Then the soldier said, "Old maid, I am dry as dust; boil me a kettle of water, will you, so that I can have several drinks of warm water and milk soon."

So the maid put the kettle on. She had secretly warned the soldier that as soon as the robbers stepped on each others' toes under the table, he had to watch out.

They started playing cards, and after a while the soldier saw that one robber stepped on the other's toes.

It's time for action, the soldier thought, and he hit the lamp so hard that the light went out.

"Take cover," he shouted to the gentleman, and he immediately started to throw the boiling water from the kettle. Then he grabbed his sabre and killed the robbers one by one.

When he had finished, he called for the old maid and said, "Would you please clean up this mess a bit, old maid, so that we can relax and talk for a while?"

So it happened, and the gentleman said, "My goodness, you're some kind of fighter! If it were not for you, this could have ended in a disaster. Please let me give you some good advice for tomorrow: I would keep that stone in your pocket, if I were you."

"No way," the other said. "That stone is for the king if I don't get a pension."

Although they went to bed late that evening, the next morning they got up early. Together they walked to the city, where the soldier entered the first inn he found and the gentleman went home.

The same morning the king summoned his prime minister and said, "I don't like to receive people just this moment; so if people come to see me, you talk to them instead. If it so happens that former soldiers come asking for a pension, tell them that they can forget it."

When the soldier learned at the inn how late the king was giving an audience, he went to the palace. He asked for an audience, and a lackey bought him to the hall where the prime minister resided. The prime minister was wearing such a dignified uniform that the soldier naturally assumed he was dealing with the king, all the more so because the prime minister did not say he was mistaken. So the soldier started telling about his many years in the service of the king, and how he was dismissed and had to suffer poverty if the king wouldn't grant him a pension. The prime minister remembered what the king had ordered, though, so he said he was sorry, but he could not give him a pension. Now the soldier asked if he had to die from hunger. Why were his past brave deeds not worth a reward anymore? The prime minister replied that so many things had to be paid for, and that there was no money left in the treasury for pensions. Then the soldier asked once more, if the king refused to give him a pension. The prime minister answered that under no circumstances would he get a pension. Then the soldier took the stone out of his pocket and threw it right in the face of the prime minister. Of course this incident lead to immediate upheaval, and the soldier was arrested and put in jail in no time.

Still, the soldier's adventure would come to a better end than he could ever have hoped for. It seems the king heard what had happened, and he knew about the brave conduct of the soldier in the home of the robbers the previous night. The king ordered the soldier to be brought before him. Imagine the soldier's astonishment, as he saw that the king and the gentleman from last night were one and the same person! Of course the soldier was highly rewarded for saving the king's life, and he was allowed to stay and live at the king's court until he died.

This story is a version of ATU 952, *The King and the Soldier*. It was told to collector C. Bakker on April 2, 1903, by an anonymous ninety-year-old storyteller from Uitdam (North Holland). The translation is based on G. J. Boekenoogen, "Nederlandsche sprookjes en vertelsels," *Volkskunde* 17 (1905): 103–106.

THE HOUSE WITH THE HEADS

*O*nce upon a time there lived a rich family on the Keizersgracht in Amsterdam. One evening the master of the house took his family out, leaving the servants to care for the mansion. It so happened that the male servant was absent too, so both the maids decided to lock all doors and windows just to be on the safe side. After serving supper, the kitchen maid, called Anna, noticed that the carving knife was a little blunt. That's why she went to the kitchen to sharpen it with the knife sharpener. Once there, after Anna had sharpened the knife, the girls clearly heard male voices coming from the basement. The second girl did not think twice and left the mansion in a hurry. Anna, however, stayed and heard the thieves (who probably had let themselves into the cellar) debating how to enter the mansion. They had discovered a trapdoor that gave way to the kitchen. They decided to climb through the trapdoor one after another, whereupon the next man was to ask, "Are you there?" If the answer was "Yes," the next would climb in, until all seven of them would be inside. Then the raiding and pillaging could begin.

Anna stood near the trapdoor, as white as a sheet, but determined to use the large, sharp carving knife she had clasped in her hand. As soon as the first robber put his head through the trapdoor, she cut off his head resolutely, then pulled the body through the hatch and put it aside swiftly. When a low voice asked, "Are you there?", she answered "Yes!" in a manly voice.

Thereupon number two followed, and so forth. Number seven, however, thought there was something fishy going on, so he fled. Not long after that, the family returned home. Horrified, they listened to the adventure about the robbers and, with great admiration, they learned about Anna's brave conduct. The master gave Anna a beautiful diamond ring as a reward. He had the heads of the six robbers cut out in stone and had them attached to the façade, so that everyone would remember the maid's loyal and heroic behaviour when passing the mansion.

(Some people say that this is the end of the story, but I know there is a sequel to it, and I will now tell it.)

A few years later, Anna was still serving the same family, who honoured her and held her in high esteem. One day the family hired a new male servant. Soon this servant, called Piet, tried to gain Anna's favours, in which he succeeded. He proposed to her and got her consent. Then he suggested asking for a day off to meet his parents. Anna agreed. They

---

asked the family for permission, and it was decided that the couple could get a full week off. So Anna and her lover left in a gig.

After they had left the city and driven for several hours, Anna asked, "Aren't we there yet?"

An anxious premonition took control of her.

"Not yet, not yet," was the answer.

After she had asked the same question several times, Piet replied, "Are you longing for your death so eagerly?"

Anna stared at him in utter amazement, and he continued, "You have killed my brothers, and now you'll have to pay for it."

Immediately she understood that he must have been the one robber who escaped, since she had already grasped that there were seven thieves, whereas only six came through the hatch. They were driving at lightning speed. At last she saw a large house; this must be the robbers' den and the place where his parents lived. They were keeping an inn, and they secretly killed all the unfortunate travellers who stayed for the night, cowardly robbing them of their money and possessions.

Anna was lifted from the wagon and handed over to Piet's parents, who immediately tied her up and locked her in a chamber. Now she had some time to think things over. Not for a moment had she lost her presence of mind; as she was being tied up, she expanded all of her muscles, so that the ropes were less tight than intended. Above all, she still wore her diamond ring. She had never shown the ring to Piet, and today she had turned the stone inside her hand, so it would not attract any attention. While she was thinking of a way to escape, with her sharp hearing she overheard the villains discussing whether they should kill her tonight or tomorrow. Her fiancé Piet was in favour of killing her that same evening, because he was well aware of her fighting spirit and bravery. Father, mother, and the other robbers preferred the next evening, because they had to attend to other business that night. The screaming of victims that Anna could hear made it perfectly clear to her that she should use every means possible to escape. She succeeded in cutting through the ropes with her diamond. She discovered a small window, which she managed to open far enough to escape. With sheets tied together, she lowered herself into a shallow ditch.

Once free, she ran until she arrived at a farm. Luckily the farmer used to deliver hay to her master every once in a while, and she begged him to hide her and take her to Amsterdam as soon as possible. Since the farmer had just prepared a colossal hay cart to take to Amsterdam the next morning, Anna decided to hide in the hay. She asked the farmer to create some room for her in the middle of the cart, just behind his back. She sat down there in a manner that she could not be lifted with a large pitchfork. Now the farmer went to bed and left early next morning. What Anna had already feared, happened. After riding along the main road for a while, some robbers appeared, dressed as farmers. They demanded that the farmer stop and unload his cargo of hay. The farmer refused, but allowed them to stab into the hay with a large pitchfork three times. If there was really someone hiding in the hay, there would be blood on the pointy ends of the pitchfork, and then he would be willing to unload. Actually, the ignorant appearance of the farmer, as well as his proposal, took away much of their suspicion. Still, they stabbed the hay thrice with all their might, but not a drop of blood was found on the end of the pitchfork. So they let the farmer go, and he kept on driving until they arrived in Amsterdam in the evening.

Anna left her hiding place and returned to the family, who received her with surprise and took care of her with love. At first she was unable to speak, because of her frightful experience, but after a while she could tell the whole story. It was decided to be extra cautious now. The police were warned, and everybody waited for the things to come. After a week, the servant returned as if nothing were wrong, and he told them that Anna had become ill and had stayed with his parents a while longer. Everyone pretended to believe him; they brought him upstairs and suddenly confronted him with Anna. He was a bit startled, but still remained cool. He was arrested and taken to prison. The robber's den was found and exterminated thanks to Anna's testimony. After that, Anna continued to live with the family in peace.

And that is as far as the story goes . . . .

This is a version of folktale type ATU 956B, *The Hot Chamber in the House of Robbers*. The story was sent to collector G. J. Boekenoogen on April 16, 1892, by Mrs. M. A. Ferwerda from Amsterdam. She claims that she heard the story from her grandmother. Although we are dealing with a well-known international (realistic) tale, the fact that the story is precisely located makes it look like a legend. "The House With the Heads" (in Dutch, "Het Huis met de Hoofden") really exists and is located at 123 Keizersgracht in Amsterdam. The six stone heads on the façade are not robbers though, but characters from classical mythology: Apollo, Diana, Ceres, Bacchus, Mars, and Minerva. In the imagination of ordinary folk, unfamiliar with classical mythology, they are the heads of the robbers. The translation is based on T. Meder and C. Hendriks, *Vertelcultuur in Nederland* (Amsterdam, 2005), pp. 138–141.

THE SOLDIER OF BARRAHUIS

*O*nce upon a time there were a farmer and his wife, who lived on a farm called Barrahuis.

One evening a soldier on horseback arrived, looking for shelter for the night. The farmer let him in, while the horse was brought to the stable.

A little while later a woman knocked at the front door. She asked for lodgings as well.

"Come on in," the farmer said.

The woman entered the farm and joined the company.

Some time later, the soldier took the farmer aside and said, "There is something suspicious about that woman, if you ask me."

"What makes you say that?" the farmer asked.

"I don't think it's a woman at all," the soldier answered. "Have you got any apples?"

"Sure," the farmer said.

"Well, just throw us each one," the soldier said, "so I can tell if I'm right."

The farmer went off to get some apples and threw an apple to everyone present. The "woman" put her knees together while catching. The soldier had seen enough; it was a man in disguise.

Moments later, the farmer said to the soldier, "We're in trouble."

The soldier said, "Don't worry. I will handle this problem."

After they went out to feed the cattle, the soldier said to the farmer, "Go inside the house again and tell everyone that I will be sleeping in the stable."

Then the soldier took off his uniform, stuffed it with straw, and lay it on the floor with a blanket on top. Now it looked as if he was sound asleep next to his horse.

As the farmer entered the house again, he said, "The soldier is already sleeping in the stable with the horses."

However, the soldier was hiding in a dark corner, biding his time . . . .

Later on, the "woman" went to the barn. The farmer had told "her" to sleep in the hay. The "woman" went over there, but as soon as the farmer had gone, "she" immediately crossed the threshing floor, without making any noise. Sneaking towards the soldier's horse, "she" found the "soldier" sleeping and stabbed "him" to death.

After that, "she" walked outside and blew on a whistle.

However, the farmer and the soldier were already waiting on the threshing floor for things to happen.

After the whistle sounded, four or five robbers approached the farm. As soon as they entered the door of the barn, the soldier killed them one after the other, including the "woman."

The next day he left on his horse again without even telling anyone his name. The farmer of Barrahuis and his wife never knew who he was. That's why he was called the unknown soldier. In honour of the soldier, the couple had a statue made of him and put it in their garden.

This is a version of the folktale type formerly known as VDK 958G*, *De appelvangproef* (The Apple Catching Test), now known as ATU 958F*, *Test of Sex: Catching an Apple*. The tale was told by the Frisian farmer and storyteller Foppe de Vries on March 8, 1968, in Garijp (province of Friesland), and was recorded by collector A. A. Jaarsma (unpublished; Jaarsma Collection, report 354, tale no. 9; archive and Dutch Folktale Database, Meertens Instituut, Amsterdam).

The Flying Dutchman

Traditional Dutch windmill in Putten (province of Gelderland). Photo by Theo Meder

Rozina

Anansi the spider and his creditors

Lily-White and the bear

Scene from the traditional fairy tale "Bluebeard"

The captured mermaid of Edam

**Representation of a White Woman in Zwiep (province of Gelderland).
Photo by Theo Meder**

The two guards

The devil visiting *The Flying Dutchman*

The godless woman and the devil

Part 5

TALES OF THE STUPID DEVIL OR OGRE

STRONG TOBACCO

*T*here once was a soldier standing guard, carrying a rifle. The devil was passing by.

"Boy," the devil said, "what a beautiful tobacco pipe you have there."

"Thanks," the soldier said, "would you like to have a drag?"

"Oh boy, I sure would," the devil said.

Then the soldier put the barrel of the rifle in the devil's mouth and pulled the trigger.

"Ugh! That's awfully strong tobacco," the devil said, and he spat out the bullet.

This version of ATU 1157, *The Ogre and the Gun*, was told in Dokkum (Friesland) by farmhand Pieter Tjeerds van der Galiën on September 8, 1971, and was recorded by collector A. A. Jaarsma (unpublished; Jaarsma Collection, report 881, tale no. 1; archive and Dutch Folktale Database, Meertens Instituut, Amsterdam).

THE STONE OWL-BOARDS

*N*ear the city of Leeuwarden there lived a farmer, who didn't have two halfpennies to his name. His farm had fallen into decay and would probably collapse in the next storm. The farmer was desperate.

One evening he was standing in his farmyard as a gentleman strolled by.

"You look depressed," the gentleman said.

"I am depressed," the farmer replied, and he told him how awful the situation was and that he was desperately short of money.

"I've got a solution to your problem," the gentleman said. "I will give you a new farm. I am the devil. The farm will be built tonight. Tomorrow morning, before the rooster crows, it will be completed. However, I need to have your soul in return."

The farmer said, "Let it be so."

Thereupon a contract was signed on the condition that the devil should have finished the farm before the rooster would crow the next morning. If the devil did not succeed, the deal was off.

After the devil had left, the farmer started having second thoughts. What had he done? He would lose his soul! He started worrying, and his wife noticed.

At first, he didn't want to tell what was wrong, but in the end he told her. Fortunately, his wife was clever.

She said, "Leave everything to me."

As they went to bed, the sounds of building and hammering had already started.

After this had continued for quite a while, the farmer's wife said: "Go and have a look how far they are."

"The walls are up already," the farmer replied.

Some time later, the woman asked, "How far are they now?"

"They are beginning to thatch the roof," the farmer answered.

A little while later, she asked once more, "How far is it now?"

The farmer said, "They only need to place the owl-boards."*

"Good," she said, and she immediately began to crow at the top of her voice.

The rooster heard it and answered at once.

The new farm was finished with the exception of the owl-boards. The woman had outwitted the devil.

Then the devil came to the house, and he was really angry.

"Never ever," he said, "will it be possible to fix an owl-board on this farm."

Well, he was right there. No owl-board would remain in place. At least . . . no wooden ones. In the end, however, they placed a stone one that didn't fall off. That's why the farm was named "the stone owl-boards."

*Frisian wooden ornaments on the rooftop.

This story has been found in Friesland in many variations. In his type-index, Jurjen van der Kooi called it VDK 1191A*, *Voor de haan kraait boerderij bouwen* (building a farm before the rooster crows). In the new international catalogue it has become tale type ATU 810A*, *The Priest and the Devil*. The story was told to collector A. A. Jaarsma around 1965 by Mrs. Geeske Kobus-Van der Zee from Nijega (Friesland). The translation is based on T. Meder, *De magische vlucht* (Amsterdam, 2000), pp. 115–116.

Part 6

TRADITIONAL LEGENDS

WHY THE WATER IN THE NORTH SEA IS SALT

*B*ecause all seawater is salt, one might say.

That's no explanation, though.

Learned men claim that they can tell us exactly why, and they use colossally elaborate and incomprehensible formulas to prove it.

Perhaps they are right, but there are people who claim that the explanation is much simpler.

As a matter of fact, there once was a tremendously big ship called *Sinternuiten.** The ship was so big that, if it lay at anchor, the stem was situated near Texel,** while the helm got stuck in the Damrak of Amsterdam.***

That's how monstrously big the ship must have been. Where it came from, nobody knew, but the fact is that the ship existed.

The ship was as long as the road from Texel to Amsterdam, perhaps even longer, because it took a horseman six weeks to ride from the front of the ship to the back.

When the captain gave his orders, it was quite an event. In those days the telephone did not exist, and they hadn't thought of signaling with flags. Imagine, if one had to sail such a sizeable ship, who would have thought of using little flags? No, the captain used to shout out his orders, obviously, and the boatswain blew his whistle as usual, but well . . . before everyone aboard was well aware of what had to happen, six weeks had passed.

So, it could well happen that the order to sail was given on the first of January, and the ship effectively left the shore in mid-February. These delays were typical—kind of a pathetic situation, isn't it?

Finally, the ship wrecked and went to the bottom of the sea—as was to be expected. It perished in the middle of the North Sea, the whole crew drowned, and the entire shipload of salt went down into the waves.

Now you understand why the North Sea, which used to be full of fresh water and swarmed with perch and carp, is so salty nowadays.

Never mind what the scholars say.

**The first Dutch island north of North Holland.

***A distance of over a hundred kilometres (approximately 62 miles).

This story is an etiological tale (explaining why the sea is salt) as well as a tall tale (about a ship of impossible magnitude). Several tale types can be attached to this story: SINUR 7B, *Warum das Meer zalzig ist* (Why the sea is salty); ATU 565, *The Magic Mill*; and ATU 1960H, *The Great Ship*. In other versions of the tall tale, storytellers expand upon the greatness of the ship, by saying for instance that men who climb the mast go up as beardless boys and come down as grey-bearded men. The translation is based on S. Franke, *Legenden langs de Noordzee* (Zutphen, 1934), pp. 105–106.

WHY FEBRUARY ONLY
HAS 28 DAYS

*I*n the early days of creation, when the months were still young, they loved to play cards with each other. February especially was fond of card playing, but he was so unlucky in the game that he always lost.

One day he noticed that he had now lost everything; but he wanted to give it one more try, and he hoped to win back his entire loss in one game.

So he started to play with his brothers January and March. Once more, luck was not on his side; he lost again, but since he didn't own a penny to pay his debts, he had to give up a day to each of his fellow players.

That is why January and March have thirty-one days and February was left with only twenty-eight days for himself.

This legend is known as folktale type SINUR 9E*, *Warum der Februar 28 Tage hat* (why February only has twenty-eight days), and was collected in the province of North Brabant. The translation is based on J. R. W. Sinninghe, *Volkssprookjes uit Nederland en Vlaanderen* (Den Haag, 1978), p. 125.

WHY THE PIGS ROOT
IN THE MUD

*O*nce upon a time there were an old woman and a young woman who lived together. One day the young woman said to the old woman that she really would
like to eat pancakes some time.

"Well," the old woman said, "as soon as you find a pretty penny, we will eat them."

Then the young woman started to sweep the whole house and she found a penny. After
that the old woman made batter for the pancakes and the young woman started to bake them.
However, when the pancake was done on one side, she did not know what to do.

Then the old woman said, "You'll have to throw and turn him over."

Unfortunately, when she tried that, the pancake landed on the edge of the pan and
broke in half. One half fell into the garbage can. The other half flew through the chimney,
straight into the wide, wide world.

There the pancake encountered an old man.

He said, "Pancake, you smell really nice. May I take a little bite of you?"

"No," the pancake replied. "I managed to escape an old and a young woman, and I'm
not going to let you eat me. No way."

And away flew the pancake.

He then met with a girl and a boy who went to school.

They asked the same question. "Pancake, may we take a bite of you?"

"No," the pancake said. "I just escaped an old woman and a young woman and an old
man, so I'm not going to let myself be eaten by a couple of children."

And again, the pancake flew away.

After a while, the pancake got very tired of all this flying around. He saw a pig lying on
the land, and he sat down on his head, next to his ear. Naturally, the pig asked for a bite as
well.

"No," the pancake replied. "I escaped an old woman and a young woman and an old
man and two children, and now I have to let you eat me?"

The old pig said, "Come sit a little closer to my ear; I'm a bit deaf, you know."

As soon as the pancake moved, the pig shook his head so hard that the pancake fell off and sank away into the mud. All the pigs started to root to find the pancake, but they did not succeed.

That's why all pigs are still rooting in the mud today.

This legend is known as folktale type SINUR 65A, *Warum das Schwein immer sucht* (Why the pig is always searching), as well as ATU 2025, *The Fleeing Pancake*. The tale was sent to collector G. J. Boekenoogen on January 14, 1894, by Mrs. S. C. Timmers-Groothuijs, who was born in the province of Drente but lived in Krommenie (North Holland). The story was written down in the dialect of Drente. The translation is based on T. Meder, *De magische vlucht* (Amsterdam, 2000), pp. 108–109.

THE BOULDER OF AMERSFOORT

The inhabitants of Amersfoort have the nickname "Boulder-pullers," which probably originates from the following story.

*J*t was a fact that beneath one of the squares of the small town, a colossal boulder had been buried. Some of the inhabitants were so curious about this enormous block of stone that they decided to dig it up. So it happened.

After digging for a long time, they finally stumbled upon the boulder, which happened to have the following inscription on it:

> *If you could turn me around,*
> *You would really be astounded.*

This inscription provided the curious diggers with enough motivation to try to pull the boulder over. It took them a lot of effort, but in the end they succeeded.

They looked at the boulder and found another inscription:

> *I'm so pleased—you don't know how—*
> *To lay on my pretty side now!*

This humorous legend is a version of AT 926B*, *Turning over the Block of Stone* (not in ATU). The tale was sent to collector G. J. Boekenoogen in February 1894 by J. W. Smitt, an importer and exporter of tea, who was born in Amersfoort (province of Utrecht), but who moved to Amsterdam. Amersfoort is still nicknamed "Boulder City." The boulder was pulled into the city in the seventeenth century as part of a wager, and was buried a few years after that. It was recovered in the nineteenth century, but the part about the inscriptions is fiction. The translation is based on T. Meder, *De magische vlucht* (Amsterdam, 2000), pp. 110–111.

HOW THE PEOPLE LEARNED
TO EAT POTATOES

*T*hese events took place in a time when people were unfamiliar with potatoes. In that time, there lived a minister who was kind of progressive. He tried to stimulate the people to eat potatoes and to cultivate them. He even commenced to grow potatoes on his own acre. However, the people refused to eat things they did not know, and they refused to grow them even more. Nobody fancied potatoes. Then the minister went to his land and had a sign put there. The sign said that no one was allowed to even touch the potatoes, because they were solely for royal consumption. It was royal food. Potatoes were only to be served at the king's table. The sign also mentioned how they had to be prepared. The minister put a policeman near the field as a guard; he had to see to it that no thieves would steal potatoes. However, the policeman just walked up and down a bit. One moment he was here, the other he was there, and he did not keep a really close watch. People like to do things that are prohibited. It so happened that every now and again, someone went to the field of potatoes and pulled some potatoes out of the ground, and slowly but surely the number of people doing this increased. First one person ate some potatoes, then another. That was exactly the intention of the minister. This is how he taught the people to eat potatoes, and everybody liked them so much that they started to grow potatoes themselves the next year.

This tale is a version of SINUR 127A*, *Warum die Kartoffeln "Pfarrerknolln" heissen* (Why potatoes are called minister-turnips). This legend was told on April 25, 1967, to collector A. A. Jaarsma by Mrs. Geeske Kobus-Van der Zee from Nijega (Friesland). The translation from Frisian is based on T. Meder, *De magische vlucht* (Amsterdam, 2000), p. 110.

HANSIE BRINKERS OF SPAARNDAM

A long time ago, there lived a boy in Spaarndam in the province of North Holland, whose father was a sluicer.* When he was about eight years old, his parents sent him to bring some pancakes to an old blind man, who lived in the polder** on his own. It was a beautiful autumn afternoon when Hansie Brinkers—that was the name of the boy—went on his way with a small package under his arm. For more than an hour he stayed with the old man, who appreciated his company very much. As Hansie walked back over the dike, he noticed that the tide was higher than normal. He imagined how the angry water would batter his father's solid sluice doors. He couldn't bear the thought that the water would ever break through the dike, destroying the sluices and flooding the fertile land. The revenge of the water on his father would be enormous!

While daydreaming, he walked on, looking back at the old man's house every once in a while. The red tone of the setting sun made the windows glow, as if everything was ablaze. The setting of the sun made Hansie Brinkers realize that he had stayed away too long; his long shadow on the grass slowly started to vanish into the dark. After he had quickened his steps, he suddenly heard something that made him stand still and stiff as a rod. It was the sound of seeping water. He slid down from the dike and, at the bottom, found a trickle of water coming through the dike, not over the dike. A hole, a hole in the dike! If the water would keep on flowing like this, the hole would get larger and larger, until the dike would break. If the flow of water wasn't stopped at once, Spaarndam and the surrounding area would be overtaken by disaster. Almost instinctively he put his finger in the hole, and the water stopped running.

In the beginning it took him little effort to stop the water, but eventually he grew numb with cold because of the wet grass and the humid mist hanging low over the meadows and the water. He started crying for help, but nobody could hear him. No one risked walking on the dark dike that late at night. He grew colder and colder, stiffer and stiffer, and a distinct pain went through his finger, through his hand, and finally through his entire body. He called for help and for his mother. His mother, however, had closed the door and the shutters hours ago and intended to reprimand her son next morning, because he had stayed overnight at the old man's place. Meanwhile, Hansie wasn't even able to whistle for help because his teeth were chattering with cold. Then he prayed to God for help and, not knowing what else to do, he decided to stay there until the next morning.

All night long, he sat there, leaning against the dike and trying not to fall asleep. The pain from cold and cramp turned his body numb. The night seemed to last forever. However, when the new day was dawning, a parish priest passed by over the dike, who had kept watch near the bed of a dying man all night. He found Hansie Brinkers and immediately understood what peril the people had escaped from.

---

*Someone in charge of the water level by opening or closing the wooden doors (the sluice).

**Low-lying and often reclaimed land that is kept dry by ditches, sluices, and dikes.

The legend of Hans Brinker (or Hansie Brinkers) was unknown in the Netherlands before it was invented by the American writer Mary Mapes Dodge (1831–1905) in her children's novel *Hans Brinker or the Silver Skates*, dating from 1865. By the way, in the novel it is not Hans Brinker who puts his finger in the dike, but an anonymous boy. The story became known in the Netherlands mainly through American tourists, who kept asking about the statue of the little hero who saved the country from drowning. To please the foreign tourists, a small statue was erected in Spaarndam in 1950 (although the original story took place near Haarlem). Because of its American origin, the story of Hans Brinker cannot be found in older editions of Dutch folktales and rarely in more modern editions, although nowadays most people in the Netherlands do know that Hans was the boy with his finger in the dike. It's kind of a silly story, because anyone who knows anything about Dutch dikes will understand that a finger cannot prevent flooding. Furthermore, the clear-cut heroism in the legend is a bit un-Dutch. There isn't an international folktale type for this story, although I invented TM 2603, *Hans Brinker*, for my own Dutch Folktale Database. The translation is based on Bert Sliggers, *Volksverhalen uit Noord- en Zuid-Holland* (Utrecht and Antwerp, 1980), pp. 89–90.

HERE IS THE TIME

Once upon a time there was a skipper, and when he sailed his ship along a certain spot, he heard a voice saying, "Here is the time, where is the man?" The skipper had heard this voice several times. One day he told this to the minister, who became curious and wanted to learn more about it. He asked the skipper if he could come along for once. So it happened. When the ship approached the place where the skipper used to hear the voice, the skipper called the minister. The minister came to the deck, and because of a sudden squall he fell overboard and drowned. After this, the skipper heard the voice nevermore . . . .

This very common traditional Dutch legend about fate is a version of SINSAG 1, "*Hier ist die Zeit, wo ist der Mann? Stimme aus den Wasser: Mann ertrinkt* ("Here is the time, where is the man?" Voice from the water: a man drowns). The story was told in the summer of 1972 to collector Ype Poortinga by the Frisian storyteller Mrs. Neeke Kossen-Bakker. The translation is based on Y. Poortinga, *De foet fan de reinbôge* (Baarn, 1979), p. 92.

THE MERMAID OF WESTENSCHOUWEN

*T*oday, Westenschouwen is nothing more than a few houses near the small town of Burgh in Zeeland, but in the old days it was an important seaport town. Once there was a Roman settlement there—ancient coins and artifacts have been found. The Danes and the Norsemen had paid the town a visit as well. This is why a burgh or stonghold was erected. The town arms of Burgh still remind us of that. In the golden age of Westenschouwen, which lasted until the second half of the middle ages, the following events took place—the facts linger on in faint memories though, so that I can recount the story only briefly.

One day, the fishermen of Westenschouwen caught a creature, "half human, half fish," in their nets. They brought the "beast" ashore. The creature was covered with seaweed and cried her eyes out. The whole day, until dark, people came to gaze at the creature.

The Mermaid of Westenschouwen

All of a sudden, a male voice rose from the sea. It was the merman calling his wife—he wanted her back. His plea was heard several times, but the fishermen refused to return their catch. Then the voice of the merman sounded again and he prophesized:

> *Westenschouwen, Westenschouwen,*
> *You'll regret this all your life,*
> *That you have robbed me of my wife.*
> *The town will drown and lose its power,*
> *The only remains will be the tower.*

And that's exactly what happened: The town went down into the sea and only the tower remained visible above the water.

Now, I must add that the tower was torn down in the middle of the nineteenth century and that the stones were used to build Mr. Speelman's barn in the middle of the small town of Burgh.

This legend is a version of SINSAG 31, *Die Prophezeiung des Meerweibes* (the prophesy of the mermaid). The tale was sent to the Meertens Instituut in 1937 by civil engineer H. J. Romeijn from Burgh (Zeeland), by means of Folklore Survey #2, form I 32. The translation is based on T. Meder, *De magische vlucht* (Amsterdam, 2000), pp. 116–117.

THE MERMAID OF EDAM

*I*t happened in the first years of the fifteenth century. During a severe storm, a fierce and wild creature of the sea floated into the Zuiderzee. After that, this mermaid washed into Lake Purmer through a huge hole in the dike. Here the mermaid floated around from one bank to the other, sleeping and waking. She was unable to reach the sea again, because in the meantime the hole in the dike had been closed. She did not wear clothes, but she was covered with seaweed and moss. She searched for food at the bottom of the lake.

Women and girls sailed in small boats from Edam and other places to the other side of the lake, where they went to milk the cows. These women and girls noticed the mermaid, and at first they were very frightened by her strange appearance. However, after a while, after they had seen her more often, they had the courage to surround the mermaid with their boats. They pulled her out of the water by force and took her to Edam. Over there, nobody was able to understand the mermaid's language, and she did not understand our tongue. The people took the seaweed and the moss off her and the mermaid was dressed. She started to eat our food. Still, time and again she tried to jump into the water, so she was well guarded. A lot of folks came to look at her. The people of Haarlem wanted to have her, and the people of Edam decided to present her as a gift to the city of Haarlem. There she learned how to spin. For a long time she lived in *Het Gat* in the Grote Houtstraat. When she died she was buried at the churchyard in Haarlem, because she often made the sign of the cross like a good Catholic.

On the Purmer Gate in Edam, which was demolished in 1835, there once stood the statue of a mermaid. The following words were written there:

> *This statue was erected in memory,*
> *Of what had been caught in Lake Purmer,*
> *In the year 1403.*

This legend is known as folktale type SINSAG 32, *Das gefangene Meerweib* (the caught mermaid), and was collected in Edam (North Holland). The translation is based on J. R. W. Sinninghe, *Spokerijen in de Zaanstreek en Waterland* (Zaltbommel, 1975), pp. 41–42.

THE INQUISITIVE FARMER

*T*he "aardmannetjes" or "alvermannetjes," named "kaboutermannetjes" in the Dutch province of North Brabant, are ugly and deformed dwarfs. Their height varies from two feet to the height of a four-year-old child. According to superstition, they live in caves. These people are crafty, agile, and adept at all sorts of art. They also keep hidden treasures. In our province they populated the hills on the heath lands in Zeelst as well as the hills of the heath land of Oirschot. The gnomes of Bergeik lived in the "Kattenberg" ("mountain of cats"), not very far north of the mill, and also in Riethoven in the "Duivelsberg" ("devil mountain"), and in other places in North Brabant. They feared daylight and showed themselves to noone. They only came out of their holes at night. If one were to put out some food or other for them, such as plain bread, they would perform all sorts of chores in gratitude for this simple gift. Although they were good and grateful to their benefactors, they were unrelenting enemies of their persecutors. The thick, short smoking pipes that they used according to popular belief are still frequently found in the ground. In North Brabant they are called "aardmannekespijpjes."

A farmer in Zeelst experienced how the gnomes showed themselves to nobody. He knew the gnomes frequented his bakery, for they had many times baked plain bread and rye bread for him. He had never seen them, though. He decided he wanted to spy on them one night. So between 12:00 and 1:00 at night, he went to the door of his bakery and heard the dwarfs very busy at work.

In a careful manner, he intended to look through a crack in the door. He had already squeezed his left eye shut and tried to peek through the crack with his right eye, when quite unexpectedly, he heard a squeaky voice say, "Blow his light out!"

The farmer jumped back in shock and dashed into his living room. He would now be blind for the rest of his life in the eye that had so carelessly wanted to peep at the work of the little labourers. Now he still knew nothing, and moreover, he had had to pay for his curiosity with the loss of his right eye.

This legend is known as folktale type SINSAG 65, *Zwerge wollen nicht belauert werden: Neugierigen des Auge ausgestochen* (Dwarfs do not want to be spied upon; inquisitive person gets eye poked out), and was sent to the Meertens Institute in 1937 by A. W. H. van Heel, an official from Vught (North Brabant). The translation is based on T. Meder, *De magische vlucht* (Amsterdam, 2000), pp. 117–118.

THE CHANGELING

*O*ne day in Tungelroij, a sandy hamlet of Weert, a gnome entered the house of a peasant woman. He begged her for alms, but the stingy woman gave him nothing and chased the little man outside. Some time later, when the woman wanted to take her child from its cradle to feed it, the child had disappeared, and the gnome was lying in the cradle. The gnome had such a vicious look on its face that the woman jumped back in shock. Then a gypsy woman entered her house, who gave her the following advice: The woman had to take half an eggshell, put flour and milk into it, and stir in it with a little spoon as if she was mixing dough. The woman followed her advice.

The gnome observed what she was doing and suddenly called out, "I have lived for hundreds of years, I have seen three sail axles being sawn out of one tree, but I have never seen anyone cooking in such a small kettle."

And all of a sudden, he disappeared and the child was back in its cradle.

This legend is known as folktale type SINSAG 91, *Das Wechselkind* (the changeling), and was sent to the Meertens Institute in 1953 by A. W. Fullemans, a retired teacher from Weert (Limburg). The translation is based on T. Meder, *De magische vlucht* (Amsterdam, 2000), pp. 118–119.

THE LEGEND OF THE WHITE WOMEN

*N*ot far from the small town of Lochem and the even smaller village of Zwiep, the Hill of Lochem can be found. On top of the Hill of Lochem there is a deep pit; it's the place where the ghostly "Witte Wieven" or White Women dwell, known to the locals as the White Women's Pit.

In Zwiep, just beneath the Hill of Lochem, there once lived a very wealthy farmer called Teunis. He was the owner of a large estate, containing vast farmlands, fruitful meadows, and a huge farmhouse. He did not have any sons though, just one daughter, a gorgeous girl called Johanna. She was in love with Albert, a handsome fellow, but unfortunately the son of a poverty-stricken dirt farmer. Johanna's father didn't want to have anything to do with this poor boy. He favoured a much better candidate for his daughter, Hendrik. Although he was a dull beanpole, he was at least the son of a well-to-do farmer. One day the father told Johanna that she was no longer allowed to see her beloved Albert. Worse still, she was grounded.

Imagine Albert's sorrow. One dark evening, he rode his horse up the Hill of Lochem. His mother used to warn him, "Don't go anywhere near that pit, my boy. These White Women do not want to be disturbed." However, in his current state of mind the warning did not bother him anymore. The only thing he could think of was Johanna.

Distracted by his own sad thoughts, he dangerously approached the edge of the pit, which nobody knew the depth of. Suddenly he sat straight in shock, as he realized that he had almost fallen into the abyss. At the very last moment, the white spirits—screaming like demons—took hold of Albert and his horse, dragged him down to a wood-path, and chased him off.

Once home, Albert told about his nocturnal journey and his miraculous rescue. He asked his sister Aaltje to bake the most delicious gingerbread she could make. Out of gratitude for his rescue, Hendrik returned to the hill and left the gingerbread behind on a dish.

Meanwhile, Johanna told Hendrik that it would never work out between them. Her father, however, was not ready to give up so soon, and he came up with a cunning plan. It was a suitor test. At night, by the light of the moon, both Albert and Hendrik had to drive up the hill and throw a whetting anvil* into the White Women's Pit. The first one to return would be allowed to marry his Johanna. Albert knew that he would not stand a chance, because

---

Hendrik owned a much faster horse. However, as soon as Hendrik entered the dark woods, he almost fouled his pants for fear. He threw the whetting anvil between some bushes and flew in terror.

Albert, on the other hand, went up the hill fearlessly and stopped at the edge of the pit. With an elegant swing he threw the iron tool into the depths and called out, "White Women, hereby I bring you the whetting anvil."**

Branches of the trees started to rustle in the wind; a dark cloud took the light of the moon away. White mist arose from the depths of the pit. Then there was the increasing sound of terrifying screams. Swiftly, Albert turned his horse and fled. One of the screeching White Women, who had caught the whetting anvil, started chasing him.

As he watched behind him, Albert looked into a pair of fiery eyes. The horseman rode for his life. By taking giant steps, the White Woman managed to catch up with him and clasped his neck with her chilly fingers. Albert roused his horse to speed up even more and released himself from the strangling hand.

Fortunately, in the distance he could distinguish the farm. Johanna was already waiting for him impatiently. She had opened the door of the barn for him and turned on the lights. The pounding of the hooves of Albert's horse swiftly came nearer and nearer. Then the snorting horse rushed inside over the threshing floor. With a mighty effort, Johanna immediately closed the heavy door of the barn, just before the White Woman could slip in. Emitting the most dreadful cries, and blinded by her own anger, the White Woman threw the whetting anvil in Albert's direction, but she missed her target. A moment later the iron tool vibrated in the wooden door. Albert and Johanna embraced each other with tears in their eyes.

Johanna's father kept his promise. He organized a splendid wedding for the happy couple and invited the whole family and the entire neighbourhood.

The day after the wedding party, Albert found a whetting anvil near the outer wall of the farm. It lay in a dish, exactly like the one with the gingerbread, which he had brought to the pit out of gratitude. What was this, then? Albert could not believe his eyes. The whetting anvil and the dish were made out of solid gold! So the White Women were well-disposed towards them after all, and the young couple lived happily ever after.

---

*Such a whetting anvil is called a "haarspit" in Dutch. It is a mower's tool on which the scythe could be sharpened with a small hammer while working in the field.

**In some versions of the legend, the words are in verse: "Witte Wieven Wit, hierbij breng ik oe het spit" ("White Women White, hereby I bring you the whetting anvil") .

This legend is known as folktale type SINSAG 305, *Weisse Frauen helfen den Menschen* (white women help people), and was collected in Zwiep near Lochem (province of Gelderland). The story was told in 2003 by miller, baker, and innkeeper Gé Postel. The translation is based on John Damen, "De sage van de Witte Wieven." *Kampioen* 118, no. 1 (January 2003): 62–64.

THE TALE OF ELLERT AND BRAMMERT IN ELLERTSVELD

*M*ore than 200 years ago, there lived a father and his son in a place that is still known as Ellertsveld—the Field of Ellert—in the province of Drente. These gruesome fellows, called Ellert and Brammert, lived in a hole under the ground, and they had stretched a rope over the road nearby. If someone passed, a bell would tinkle in their hideout. Then they would go out to murder their victim, and bury the stolen silver and gold somewhere under the ground.

One day a pretty girl, who was on her way to Norg, passed their hole. As soon as her feet touched the rope, Ellert ran out and put his hands around her throat. However, when he saw what a pretty thing she was, he took her along into their hideout.

Ellert and Brammert got into a row, because Brammert argued that she should have been killed. Ellert, however, wanted to keep her alive and have her as his wife. And that's exactly what happened.

The girl begged for mercy, but it did not do her any good. From that moment on, one of these awful men would always stay behind in the hole, because they were afraid she would escape.

After she had lived with them for a year, they said to each other, "Tomorrow we'll have to go out together. I suppose she will no longer run away, will she?"

As soon as they had left, though, and the girl wasn't able to distinguish them in the distance any more, she ran away as fast as her feet could carry her.

The men returned home earlier than expected, and when they saw that she had left, they ran out each in a different direction in order to catch her again. Ellert, who was a very fast runner, almost caught up with her. He threw his axe at her, but he missed; the axe hit the barn door of the farm to which she was able to flee.

In safety, the girl told everything there was to tell. Thereupon the bailiff and his officers tracked the murderers down and put them in jail. Soon after, they were beheaded.

Even today, as soon as it turns dark, you can still see ghostly White Women hovering over Ellertsveld—they were once the victims of Ellert and Brammert.

The twist at the end of the legend makes it belong to SINSAG 311, *Weisse Frau ist eine zurückgekehrte Tote* (White Woman is a wandering soul). The tale was sent to collector G. J. Boekenoogen on January 14, 1894, by Mrs. S. C. Timmers-Groothuijs, who lived in Krommenie (North Holland) but who was born in the province of Drente. The legend is especially well known in Drente, in many versions. The translation is an adaptation of the tale in dialect by Mrs. Timmers-Groothuijs as published in T. Meder and C. Hendriks, *Vertelcultuur in Nederland* (Amsterdam, 2005), pp. 334–335.

JAN WITHOUT FEAR

Many years ago, in Germany, between the town of L. and the village of B., there was an uninhabited, crumbling castle, sitting on the top of a high mountain, surrounded by shrubbery, with an extended forest at its feet. The general perception of the village was that it was haunted. For this reason, the villagers who passed by it after dark, passed in fear; if possible, they preferred a detour.

One day the villagers were informed by a traveller (who had seen it with his own eyes) that on the previous night, passing by the castle, he had seen light in one window, and also a shadow sliding by. It had given him a right shock. He had run to the village as fast as he could to tell everything to the bailiff. The bailiff then decided that some strong men should spend a night at the castle to kill the ghost. But everybody lacked the courage to do so. The villagers had become so frightened by all that had happened that from now on, coming from the town by nightfall, they made a detour to avoid going past the dreaded castle. The bailiff understood that things could not go on like this and promised twenty thalers* to whoever had the courage to spend one night at the castle. But still, nobody showed up.

Finally there came Jan the blacksmith, a sturdy, middle-aged man who had received a nickname from all who knew him for the brave deeds he had done for the village during the flooding. They called him Jan Without Fear. Having heard all that had happened, he immediately took on the assignment, whilst being cheered by the whole town. That same evening, he went on his way to the castle. With him he took a lantern, some pitchers of beer, a pot of flour, and a large hammer as his only weapon. Having arrived at the castle, he went straight to the kitchen, lit his lantern, fetched some dry wood from the shrubbery, and lit a fire in the hearth. He sat down on a bench and drank some glasses of beer. After having rested a bit, he made batter out of the flour and started baking cakes. He was completely at ease here, and without fear, as if he was in an ordinary house. He was surprised at not having seen anything of the ghost yet.

But hardly had the village clock struck midnight, when he heard a rustling noise above his head. That'll be the ghost, Jan thought, but he was still very surprised when a leg fell down the chimney, right on top of his cakes.

Oh, that's nice, he thought, and he threw it into a corner. Fifteen minutes later, another leg fell on his cakes, which he threw into the same corner. After this, there followed a trunk, two arms, and a skull, all of which Jan threw into the corner. Without being fazed by all this, he continued his baking. Just when he had finished, he heard some movement in the corner.

He turned his head and saw that the bones had arranged themselves into a complete skeleton.

The skeleton beckoned Jan to come along with him. Jan followed him, mostly out of curiosity to know what he wanted. He took his lantern along, and also his hammer, which he hid under his coat. In the corridor, the ghost opened a door that led to a subterranean vault. After having passed through several nasty, chilly vaults, the skeleton finally opened a large, heavy iron door, which led to an even darker vault. In this vault, the skeleton pointed at a large stone on the floor. Jan understood his gesture, picked up a strong old tool lying there, and used it to lift the stone and some other stones around it. After having worked at this for quite a while, he saw three large chests.

Jan then turned around to look at the ghost. It began to speak. In a disagreeable, hollow, sepulchral voice, it said, "I am the ghost of the deceased knight to whom this castle and all these treasures belonged. During my lifetime, I was known everywhere for being an old skinflint, and that is how I died. But as a punishment for my avarice, I have never found peace in my grave and must return all nights to guard over my treasures. I could not be released until a human being came here in the night and accomplish what I can no longer do, namely to divide these three chests containing all my treasures. One for the church, one for the poor, and this one for you, my rescuer, for the service you have done me. Try to make better use of it than I did. Now I can return to my grave in order and peace."

Thereupon the ghost disappeared, even before Jan had recovered from his surprise and had had the chance to thank him for what he had done. When Jan came back to the ground floor, it was broad daylight. He immediately went to see the bailiff, who was surprised to see Jan alive. Jan told him everything. The will of the deceased knight was faithfully carried out. As for Jan, he did not want to accept the promised reward of twenty thalers, so he gave the money to the poor.

Thanks to the treasure, Jan was now immensely rich. He sold off his smithy and went to lead a quiet and simple life with his wife and children in a large house. He was very good to the poor, and all the people who knew him esteemed and respected him. And in addition, ghosts were heard of no more from that moment on.

---

*A thaler is a German silver coin.

This legend is a version of SINSAG 401, *Der verborgene Schatz* (the hidden treasure). The story was sent to collector G. J. Boekenoogen on June 20, 1892, by Mrs. M. R. van der Veer from Driebergen (province of Utrecht). The translation is based on T. Meder, *De magische vlucht* (Amsterdam, 2000), pp. 120–122.

THE FLYING DUTCHMAN

Ships of the VOC* had to take a specific route from Amsterdam to Batavia** and back. In case they were damaged out at sea, the chances that they would encounter another ship were best on this route. It was called "the safe track."

*C*aptain Barend Fockesz of the swift, armed merchant ship *De Kroonvogel* did not care for safe tracks. To shorten his trips, he often left the track. While it took slow and heavy VOC ships eight to twelve months to complete a journey, Barend could do it in six months. Still, he felt the trip was taking too long, but he realized the only way he could sail faster would be with the aid of the devil. Then one night the devil became his guest out at sea, west of the Cape of Good Hope.

At night a small sloop approached *De Kroonvogel* and a gentleman, all dressed in black, came aboard. Nobody noticed, because all were asleep: the helmsman, bent over the great wheel, the sailor who had to keep watch in the crow's nest, and the navigating officer on the bridge. Only Barend Fockesz was awake and waiting. Slowly, the door of his cabin opened and the devil entered.

"You called me, Barend Fockesz?"

"Yes, I want to make even shorter journeys."

"Then you will always have to sail with full sails."

"And what if the rigging goes overboard in a storm?" Barend asked.

"Fasten the ropes and wires with iron bars, so that the yard can't go overboard. Hollow out your masts and fill them with liquid lead, and they can't break anymore," the devil replied.

"Then the ship becomes too heavy, way too heavy," Barend said.

"Oh no, with my help you will sail over reefs and rocks, over shallow water and sandbanks. Be it with head wind or no wind at all, *De Kroonvogel* will always have full sails. For centuries the seamen will speak of your ship; they will call it *The Flying Dutchman.*"

After that time, *De Kroonvogel* made even shorter trips from Amsterdam to East India. Three months after he boarded the ship, Barend Fockesz went on land at the Waterpoort in Batavia. Captain Barend was rewarded with golden commemorative medals, golden necklaces, and bags full of the finest Spanish silver and golden coins. On the uninhabited little island Kuiper, near the harbor of Batavia, they even erected a statue for him. There Barend stood, cut out in stone, dressed in a pea jacket and short trousers, so that every crew member leaving the roadstead could see him. (When in 1808 the British Admiral Dourie didn't dare to attack Batavia, because Daendels*** was in command of the city and the fortress, British sailors smashed the statue to pieces.)

On one of its fast trips, *De Kroonvogel* lost its navigating officer in the Sunda Strait. Perhaps the devil had fallen asleep for a while; in any case, the sails were hanging down from the yardarms and the ship was unable to get past the small island of Slee-Bessie. The officer navigating became so angry that he swore not to rest before he widened the waters by towing Slee-Bessie to Krakatau. His wish was granted right away. Nowadays, when the weather is calm and the waves are not too noisy, one can still hear the officer singing—as is customary among seamen—while towing one island towards the other. Sceptical people don't believe this story. They say that the strange singing one can hear in the Sunda Strait can be explained by the movement of the wind in the holes of the rocks of the island Krakatau.

The new navigating officer, who signed up in Amsterdam, was not used to reckless sailing. The first time the ship sailed over the cliffs again, he feared that soon there wouldn't be enough water to keep on floating, and he wanted to check by throwing out a lead line. However, there was no lead line on board and that's why he took a cannonball, attached it to a rope, and was about to throw it over, when Barend stopped him.

"Better trust me and the devil. We are sailing fine and we will continue to do so," he said.

That was correct, but during that journey the seven years of the contract came to an end, and the whole ship was taken over by the devil. Now *The Flying Dutchman* is sailing the seven seas for eternity, without ever entering a harbour. The ship is always sailing with full sails, be it with or against the wind. The appearance of the black ship is an omen of storm and destruction for the ships it encounters.

In the evenings, many ships have been hailed by *The Flying Dutchman* and one can clearly see the figure of the captain on the bridge. He has become very, very old now, and in his feeble, bony hand he holds a letter with black wax seals, which he wants to give to the captain of the ship he is hailing. It is a letter for the Lords Seventeen, the directors of the VOC in Amsterdam. However, no one ever dared to accept the letter.

*Verenigde Oostindische Compagnie (United East Indian Company), a rich Dutch trading company in the seventeenth and eighteenth centuries, carrying colonial merchandise such as coffee, tea, tobacco, and spices.

**Jakarta, Indonesia.

***Governor-general Herman Willem Daendels (1762–1818).

This legend is a version of SINSAG 471, *Schiff segelt durch die Luft* (Ship sailing through the air), and of ATU 777*, *The Flying Dutchman*. In fact, the tale of the doomed Dutch ghost ship stems from a British literary tradition (eighteenth to nineteenth centuries). The name of the captain varies; when he is called Willem van der Decken, he comes from Terneuzen in the province of Zeeland. Barend Fockesz (Fockesz = son of Fokke), on the other hand, was a Frisian captain, who actually managed to sail to Batavia in three months and earned a statue on the island Kuiper. The translation of the legend is based on J. R. W. Sinninghe, *Spokerijen in Amsterdam en Amstelland* (Zaltbommel, 1975), pp. 8–11.

TWO WITCHES, WHO WENT TO THE WINE CELLAR

A youthful witch once flew with a group of experienced witches from Herkenbosch in Limburg to Cologne in Germany, in order to have a few stiff drinks in a local wine cellar, well known by the elderly ladies. The witches sat down on their broomsticks, and the leader of the witches made the flight possible by using the following magic formula:

> *Hoetepetoet!*
> *Out through the chimney,*
> *Over hedge and bush,*
> *'Til in Cologne in the wine cellar,*
> *And afterwards back home.*

The young witch had such a good time in Cologne that she decided to make the trip once more, but this time just with a young friend, who had also entered the school of witchcraft only recently. They wanted to have more freedom to do as they pleased.

At first, the friend made objections, especially because the trip was a dangerous one. After all, if one did not return home before sunrise, the devil would break their necks. Still, with some smooth talk the young witch persuaded her hesitant friend to come along; not to worry, she knew the magic formula by heart.

One fine evening—it was almost midnight—both witches were fully prepared to undertake the journey. Sitting on their broomsticks, they waited for the first striking of the clock, and then the first witch said:

"Now then . . . all set?"

"Yes. I'm ready," the second witch replied.

"Right. Here we go," said the first witch.

"Wait a minute," the other witch said. "Isn't it too dangerous to fly over such a distance? Hadn't we better stay home?"

"Are you chicken?" the first witch replied. "I'm not afraid at all. I can already smell the wine, if you ask me. Now, let's go.

Hoetepetoet!
Out through the chimney,
Then through hedge and bush,
'Til in Cologne in the wine cellar,
And nevermore back home."

Obviously, the frivolous witch made a few mistakes reciting the magic formula.

They flew out of the chimney, but instead of flying high into the sky as on the last trip, they now flew just above the ground, through hedges and bushes, to the wine cellar. Heavily battered, they arrived at their destination, their heads and shoulders full of lumps and scratches, and if the fabric of their clothes had not been of such a high quality, they would have arrived half naked and even more wounded. There they lay down on the cellar floor, panting and bleeding. The second witch came to herself, and said in a moaning voice:

"You see? I told you that it could go wrong!"

After the witches had come to their senses a bit, they merrily started drinking the wine from the cellar.

"I wish we were home," the second witch said, sipping from her glass.

"Oh, come on!" the first witch said. "We will manage . . . . We still have our 'horses'. . . . Where is yours?"

"Here it is," the second witch said. "I had to hold on real tight in order not to lose it . . . . I wish we were home."

"You're a first class chicken," the first witch grumbled. "Give me your glass and I'll fill it up again."

"Okay," the other witch replied, "but that's the last one. We can't get drunk and fall off our 'horses'. In that case, we will never get home in time for sure. Brr . . . ," and she made the gesture of breaking her own neck.

"There is still time," said the first witch in a soothing manner. "Still, let's not waste it. Just one glass and then we'll go."

After they had emptied their glasses for the third time, the witches sat on their broomsticks in order to travel back home . . . but their horses remained motionless.

They shouted and groaned, turned their broomsticks back and forth, made all kinds of movements to activate the horses, but to no avail . . . .

"Now what?" the second witch moaned.

"Yes, now what?" the first witch repeated. "We are lost, absolutely lost."

"Why?" the other asked: "How can you be so sure, all of a sudden?"

"Because I can remember now," said the first witch. "I made a mistake in the magic formula. Instead of *over* I said *through* hedge and bush, and that's why the journey was so uncomfortable. However, I also said *nevermore* instead of *afterwards* back home. We are lost indeed!"

"Oh dear! Oh dear!" the other witch lamented. "I'm afraid you're right. It doesn't matter anymore; the devil will get us anyway—either now or tomorrow morning. What's the difference in the perspective of eternity? Still, I refuse to go to hell sober . . . . Fill me up!" she said, passing her glass.

"That's the first sensible thing you've said all day," the first witch said. "Let's drink, drink, drink . . . . Then at least we won't feel how the devil breaks our necks."

Then the two witches drank as much wine as they could master. It wasn't long before they both lay flat on their backs on the cellar floor—completely drunk.

As it happened, some workers came into the cellar very early that morning. They found the two witches, passed out on the floor, with their broomsticks next to them. The workers went to alarm the authorities. In no time, everyone in the entire city of Cologne was up and about. The whole population witnessed how, well before sunrise, the witches were brought to the stake and tied back to back on the pole.

Now the story is reaching its end. Fortunately the witches didn't have to experience how the devil broke their necks in the cellar. As soon as they felt the first flames licking their bodies, the witches came to their senses, and they both converted themselves to Christianity again, before they were consumed by the fire.

The devil was not amused at all, and everyone could see that: He was flying over the stake in the shape of a little owl, and the air was soon filled with the ghastly smell of sulphur and pitch. He had lost his power over the witches, and returned to hell empty handed.

This legend is known as folktale type SINSAG 511, *Über Weg und Steg* (over road and path), and was collected in 1894 in Roermond, in the province of Limburg. The translation of the text, which is partly in a dialect of Limburg, is based on Willem de Blécourt, *Volksverhalen uit Nederlands Limburg* (Utrecht and Antwerp, 1981), pp. 131–133 (N 7.1).

THE BEWITCHED SHIP

*O*nce upon a time there was a shipmaster who had a boat. He never slept in it himself, though, and neither did his servant. One day he got a new servant. When this servant got up in the morning, he saw that the ship was lying the other way round. He was sure he had not tightened the ship that way the night before.

So he told his boss, who said, "Oh, that's nothing. It happens every night. That's the reason why we don't have the stomach to spend the night in it."

"Well, I have," said the servant. That night he decided to lie awake in the fore-cabin.

That night, all of a sudden he heard a terrible racket.

Several people were walking and running across the deck, and he heard someone shouting, "Release the ropes, raise the sails, shift that helm."

And after a while, the ship sailed away. Some time later, the ship was lying still. The servant then climbed up towards the deck, put his head through the hatchway, and saw a branch of a Chinese orange tree, with Chinese oranges on it, hanging over the ship. He then saw that he was in China, broke off the branch, took it back down with him, and pretended to be asleep again.

Shortly after, he heard the same noises, the same commands, and again, the ship started moving. As soon as all was quiet once more, he had another look and saw that the ship was back in its old place at the Langendijk, for this is where it all happened.

In the morning he went to the shipmaster to tell him everything. He showed him the branch with Chinese oranges as proof.

The shipmaster's wife then said, "Well, you've been lucky that there was familiar folk among them, 'cause otherwise you wouldn't have got away with it and they would surely have killed you."

The servant found this strange and started thinking about it.

One day he asked his boss whether his wife was always home at night.

"Oh yes," he said, "but what of it?"

"Well, in that case, I would like to spend the night in your room sometime, if I may."

And so it happened.

After midnight, the wife appeared to be sleeping very quietly. Then the servant said, "Let's try and wake her up, just for the fun of it."

And so they tried. But they did not succeed, no matter what they did.

Then the servant said, "Let's put her in the bed in the other room."

And so it happened. After a while, they heard groaning, moaning, weeping, and so on.

As soon as the servant thought this had gone on long enough, he said, "Let's put your wife back in her own bed now."

Hardly had she been put back, when the moaning stopped and the wife woke up— her spirit had left her body and of course, it initially had some trouble finding its way back. When the body was lying in its original place, the spirit went back in, and then the wife woke up.

When she saw her husband and the servant, she said, "Well, are you up yet? Please hurry to bring us a cup of coffee then, because I'm sure I must have slept very soundly."

The boss and his servant, however, had heard and seen enough. The wife was a witch and it was under her command that the ship went to China every night.

This legend belongs to folktale type SINSAG 513, *Die verzauberte Jacht* (the bewitched yacht). The story was taken down on May 18, 1911, from an anonymous storyteller from Zuiderwoude (North Holland), by collector C. Bakker. The translation is based on T. Meder, *De magische vlucht* (Amsterdam, 2000), pp. 124–125.

THE BEWITCHED MILL

*O*nce upon a time there was a miller who had a mill that would not turn. No matter what people tried, there was just no way to get it going. The miller could not keep any servants, for they either fled from the mill in fear at night, or they died of fright after having spent some time in it. One day, a beggar turned up at the miller's doorstep.

"Do you want to help me grind?" said the miller, "you can make a lot of money doing so."

Of course the beggar was willing.

"Well, you should know that there is some terrible life in the mill every night and that we just can't get it to turn."

"Oh, I'm not afraid of that. Just let me watch out there," said the servant, "but make sure you put a burning candle on every step of the stairs up till the last rung on the top."

So it happened. At first the miller and the servant were sitting by the fire in silence, but when it became late night, they suddenly heard some thumping and tumult. All the candles were blown out one by one, and a troop of black cats entered the mill.

When the cats got to the table, and intended to blow out the candle on it as well, the beggar said, "That's enough, pussycats, I wouldn't do that if I were you, because it would take all our sight away. Why don't I make us a nice cup of coffee, so we can have a nice chat."

This was only an excuse, for he needed the boiling water for something else. So the cats sat by the fire, and by Jove, they started talking.

"I'm off," said the miller.

"No, no," said the beggar, "you must stay."

After having sat like that for a while, one cat said to another, "I think we should chuck him out."

Some time later, the cat repeated this.

"Be careful," said the miller, "for they have already topped quite some guys. I'm off."

Again the cats said, "We should chuck him out of here."

But then one cat said, "Let's wait for Ginger first."

Some time later, a ginger cat came rushing in.

This is the time to spring to action, the beggar thought. He took a wooden spoon and started throwing the boiling water over the cats.

Howling and screaming, the cats fled, and from that moment on, the mill started grinding. When the miller got up in the morning, the beggar had already ground a few sacks full. But the worst was yet to come, for the miller's wife was covered with blisters. She had had a hand in it, for she was a witch, you see.

This legend belongs to folktale type SINSAG 622, *Die verzauberte Mühle* (the bewitched mill). The story was taken down on April 2, 1903, from an anonymous, ninety-year-old storyteller from Uitdam (North Holland), by collector C. Bakker. The translation is based on T. Meder, *De magische vlucht* (Amsterdam, 2000), pp. 126–127.

THE CAT FAIR

*S*omewhere in the country, a troop of cats was having a fair. Nobody dared disturb them, though, for they were all afraid of witchcraft.

As it happened, a golden candlestick had been stolen from a church in that same area.

The next year, the people decided to keep an eye on the cats. When the day in question came, they were on the lookout in the area. To their horror, they saw the candlestick where the cats were. How on earth were they to get it back? One of them proved brave enough. He went to the field and greeted the cats. Then he grabbed the candlestick and wanted to leave. But the cats asked him to stay for a little while. So he did, and the cats all went to the fire, and pretended to be forced into a kettle full of oil, which was hanging over a large fire. The man had pity on them and moved closer to the fire.

Now the cats said:

> *"Do we wanna wettle,*
> *do we wanna wettle,*
> *do we wanna put him with his head*
> *into the kettle?"*

Then they put him with his head into the oil. He ran away fast, but forgot to take the candlestick along.

The man became very ill and spent some six weeks in bed. After that, he regained the strength to do some walking. But all the time he had been ill, he kept hearing the cats meowing.

One morning his wife went out. So he stayed home alone, but told his wife to put the kettle on. So she did, and left. The water was boiling, and now the man went out and called the cats in. Then he walked towards the water and threw it over the cats.

In the morning it was heard that all the old women had burnt themselves and that one of them had even been killed.

This is believed to be true, and it explains the origins of the cat fair.

This legend contains several folktale types: SINSAG 640, *Hexentier verwundet: Frau zeigt am folgenden Tag Malzeichen* (witch hurt as animal; woman turns out to be wounded the next day); SINSAG 501, *Der Katzentanz* (the cat's dance); and SINSAG 503, *Die gestörte Hexenversammlung* (the meeting of witches disturbed). The story was sent to collector G. J. Boekenoogen in March 1892 by teacher C. J. Kieviet of Oosthuizen (North Holland). The translation is based on T. Meder, *De magische vlucht* (Amsterdam, 2000), pp. 127–128.

JACK OF CLUBS GETS JENEVER

A storyteller from Zuiderwoude* personally experienced the following events. When he was a soldier, he had to keep watch with several other soldiers. As a pastime they played cards.

Suddenly, one of the soldiers said, "Shall I send the jack of clubs for a bottle of jenever**?"

Everyone laughed, because they thought it was a joke, but when he persevered and asked them all to contribute a dime, they decided to take the risk.

One, two, three, there, it happened! The jack of clubs disappeared, the soldier fell unconscious, he turned as white as a sheet, and he started sweating like a pig. After a few minutes, a bottle of jenever appeared on the table, with the jack of clubs around the neck. It can't be explained how this was possible.

Immediately the soldier regained consciousness. Nobody dared to take a drink from the bottle, but when the soldier drank the first glass with apparent delight, the others lost their fear and they emptied the bottle together.

The next day, one of the guards at the main gate told them that someone had delivered him such a blow that he almost passed out. However, when he looked around to see who had slapped him, he saw no one at all. When the soldiers went out to march that day, they came across an innkeeper who lived some fifteen minutes outside town.

He said to them, "You sure made a lot of noise last night, just to get me out of bed in the middle of the night for a bottle of jenever."

Everyone denied having done this, all the more so because the innkeeper mentioned that the bottle of jenever was not paid for. The innkeeper maintained that he was telling the truth, and he pointed out the soldier who sent out the jack of clubs as the one who came for the bottle.

My storyteller ended his tale by saying, "Certainly, that soldier must have been a sorcerer, whose ghost was able to leave his body. He never left the room, and no ordinary person could have made it to the inn and back in just a few minutes."

---

*A small village in Waterland in the province of North Holland. The name of the storyteller is unknown.

**Jenever is Dutch gin.

This legend belongs to folktale type SINSAG 685, *Pikbube als Helfer. Spielkarte ausgeschickt, um Schnaps zu holen* (Jack of clubs as helper; playing card send out to fetch liquor). The story was taken down on April 23, 1901, by collector C. Bakker. The translation is based on T. Meder, *De magische vlucht* (Amsterdam, 2000), pp. 130–131.

THE WITCHES IN THE SIEVE

A farmhand went to the Mheen (the Arkemheen polder near the villages of Putten and Nijkerk) to take the horses in. In the distance, he heard some beautiful singing, which gradually came closer. He saw two women in a sieve coming from the sky. As soon as they had landed, they hid the sieve in the reeds and the rushes. Then they each sat on a horse and trotted like mad through the meadow. Big flakes of foam fell from the horses' mouths. The farmhand secretly walked towards the sieve and hid it. When the women finally returned, they went looking for the sieve.

When they could not find it, they noticed the farmhand and asked, "Have you seen a sieve around here?"

"No."

"You did see it, and then you hid it, mate!"

"No."

"You have to give it back to us or show us where it is. We have to go. It is our time. Remember, if we are not back within the hour, we will be pinched and beaten black and blue."

"Don't be silly."

"No, really. You have to give it back to us. If you do, we will give you a nice silk cloth."

"There is the sieve."

The women hurried into it, made a sign, muttered something, and flew through the sky as quickly as they had arrived.

A few days later, the farmhand found the promised silk cloth in the place where he had spoken with the women.

This legend is known as folktale type SINSAG 782, *Das gefundene Sieb* (the found sieve), and was sent to collector G. J. Boekenoogen on April 18, 1892, by H. Baarschers from Amsterdam (North Holland). The translation is based on T. Meder, *De magische vlucht* (Amsterdam, 2000), pp. 132–133.

THE WEREWOLF

*J*n a house in the middle of the forest there once lived three religious souls: a father, a mother, and their daughter. On the door of their house hung a Saint Andrew's cross, as a defence against devils, ghosts, and other supernatural dangers; because of the cross they would not be able to enter the house.

One evening the parents had to go out, and they told their daughter not to open the door to anyone. Of course, the parents were very worried that they had to leave their daughter behind, all alone in the house in the middle of the vast forest.

The daughter, however, was glad that they left, because now she could finally invite her secret boyfriend over. Until that time, she locked all the doors and windows. She wasn't really afraid, because she was sure the cross on the door would protect her.

Suddenly she heard a fearful scream somewhere outside. She went out into the forest to see what was going on. Soon the girl was sorry, because her red skirt got soiled, which she would be unable to explain, since it was forbidden to leave the house.

Then she heard rustling sounds in the bushes and as she looked to the side, she saw a werewolf running towards her. She ran back to the house in terror. The werewolf almost caught up with her, and he even tore a piece of her skirt with his sharp teeth. Just in time the girl reached the house, where she would be safe because of the cross. She slammed the door behind her and locked up. The werewolf left soon after.

Once she had calmed down, the girl changed clothes. After a while her boyfriend knocked on the door. She opened the door and told him what had happened. He didn't believe a word she said, and he roared with laughter. Now what did she see? Between his teeth she saw pieces of red cloth from her skirt . . . . It almost scared her to death.

This is as far as the story goes, I'm afraid.

This legend is known as folktale type SINSAG 823, *Das zerbissene Tuch* (the bitten cloth), and was sent to me by Moniek Grimme from Oirschot (North Brabant) on October 4, 1998. The translation is based on T. Meder, *De magische vlucht* (Amsterdam, 2000), pp. 134–135.

THE GODLESS WOMAN

*I*n a house in a small town there used to live a man. He was the richest farmer in the entire neighbourhood, and he had a lot of farmhands and maids. One of these maids had already reached a certain age . . . but no young man desired her for a bride, because her ability to curse and raise hell scared them all.

One day, when there was a fair, she said to herself, "If I can't get a boyfriend tonight, I will go out with the devil."

Truly, that evening she met a handsome young man. They had a lot of fun together, and later that night the young man escorted his girlfriend home. He came inside as well. However, he stayed so long that the maid became frightened. She warned the owner, and he quickly sent someone out with a message for the minister.

When the minister arrived, he tried to convince the man to leave. Despite friendly words, the stranger refused to go. Everything they tried was in vain. At his wit's end, the minister started to pray the Lord's Prayer. As he reached the verse "release us from all evil," the stranger disappeared all of a sudden.

People say, it must have been the devil.

The tale is a version of SINSAG 902, *Teufel tantzt mit Mädchen, das tanzen will, wenn es auch mit dem Teufel wäre* (Devil dances with girl who wants to dance, even if he were the devil). The legend was sent to collector G. J. Boekenoogen at the end of the nineteenth century by C. W. Pisuisse, who lived in Lutten (province of Overijssel). The translation is based on T. Meder and C. Hendriks, *Vertelcultuur in Nederland* (Amsterdam, 2005), p. 252.

THE WOMAN OF STAVOREN

Once there was a very rich widow, who lived in Stavoren in the province of Friesland. She owned a lot of ships that sailed the seven seas to trade in far away countries.

One day she said to one of her shipmasters, "Now bring me the most beautiful thing in the world that money can buy."

After a long journey, the shipmaster returned with a shipload of rye.

The widow was furious. She said to the shipmaster, "Are you out of your mind? Do you think this is the most beautiful thing in the world?"

Next, she asked, "How did you load it? From larboard?"

"From larboard," the skipper confirmed.

"It came in from larboard," she said. "Now you can throw it out into the sea from starboard."

So it happened.

From the quay, a grey old man observed what was going on, and he said to the widow, "One day, you will be poor."

"You fool," she said to the grey old man, "get lost. I cannot become poor anymore."

She took the golden ring from her finger and threw it into the sea.

"No more than I will ever regain this ring, no more will I be poor."

Fourteen days later, a fishmonger came into town. The widow bought some fish. When she cut open the first fish, she fainted because of the shock: Inside the fish she saw her golden ring. The fish had swallowed it.

Next, violent storms came with thunder and lightning. All of her ships at sea were lost. Parts of the dikes were washed away. All of her wealth she lost to the sea. In the end, she had to survive by begging.

After all this time, you can still see where the rye went overboard. Every year, stalks of grain are growing out of the water, but they remain empty.

This tale contains the folktale types SINSAG 1121, *Gottes Gaben nicht geachted* (God's gifts not appreciated) and ATU 736A, *The Ring of Polycrates*. The story was told in Drachten (Friesland) by the working-class storyteller Hendrik Meijer on April 10, 1969, and was recorded by collector A. A. Jaarsma (unpublished; Jaarsma Collection, report 623, tale no. 7; archive and Dutch Folktale Database, Meertens Instituut, Amsterdam).

CHILDRENSDIKE

*I*t all happened during the Saint Elisabeth's Flood, November 18, 1421. The waves washed over the low lands in a fury, and everywhere dikes were swept away as if they were made of paper. People and cattle drowned and died a miserable death. Cries of despair were heard all over the land.

But what does the sea care for lamentations? The water ran through the huge holes in the dikes and swept away all that it encountered. The people in no less than seventy-two villages near the city of Dordrecht drowned. The fertile soil changed into a vast stretch of salt water. Where once the area had been vital and productive, there now remained the Biesbosch, with its creeks and its inlets.

Certainly this is what happened during the days of the Saint Elisabeth's Flood. Nothing remained of the seventy-two prospering villages. Houses and churches, people and cattle, were all swallowed up by the sea.

It so happened that in these days *one* miracle occurred.

One human life was spared.

As far as the eye could see, there was water—there were waves everywhere. All that once lived, had gone under; but see, what was floating over there? That tiny dot over there, that object that rocked on the waves? Was it a cradle?

By all means, it was a cradle, and there was a tiny, rosy child lying in it. It sucked its little thumb, and its blue eyes looked at the grey sky in an innocent way.

How was it possible that the cradle didn't turn over? How could it be that the waves did not wash it away?

The answer was a cat on the hood of the cradle, jumping from left to right and back again, thus keeping the strange vessel in balance.

Where did the cradle come from, and whatever happened to the child?

Nobody knows, but up until today, the very spot where the cradle came ashore is called *Kinderdijk*—Childrensdike.

This legend is known as folktale type SINSAG 1172, *Die Katze auf der Wiege, hält die Wiege im Gleichgewicht* (the cat on the cradle, keeping the cradle in balance), and was collected in the province of South Holland. The translation is based on S. Franke, *Legenden langs de Noordzee* (Zutphen, 1934), pp. 119–120.

THE HERRING IN THE BUCKET

When the Dollard was not there yet, there was a large farm in the neighbourhood of Termunten. One morning the farmer drew water from the well for his cattle.

To his utter amazement, he saw a herring swimming in the bucket. He kept on scratching his head over this matter. Finally he concluded that the fish must have swum through the earth into the well. That could only mean that the sea was seeping under the land. One autumn storm, and all the land would be swept away by the sea!

The entire summer the farmer walked around with this secret. The man completely lost his sense of humour. A snap and a snarl was all he was good for.

He sold the farm and moved to another place, on higher ground. He could not find any peace of mind, though. He could not sleep at night. In the daytime, he sat in his yard for hours, just staring.

As the first autumn storm came, the inevitable happened.

That same stormy night the farmer was found dead in his barn.

This legend is known as folktale type SINSAG 1173, *Der Hering im Brunnen* (the herring in the well), and was collected by K. ter Laan in the province of Groningen. The translation is based on E. de Jong and P. Klaasse, *Sagen en Legenden van de Lage Landen* (Bussum, 1980), p. 27.

THE FALL OF TIDDE WINNENGA

*T*he farmers of Reiderland were the richest farmers of Groningen. The richest of them all was Tidde Winnenga.

One day a severe storm was rising. Everybody worked to strengthen the dike, except Tidde. His farm stood on higher ground, so he didn't worry.

The neighbours urged him to help; the entire land was in great danger. Tidde Winnenga was stubborn. He would not leave his farm, he said, until the water on his land was six feet high.

The dike broke, and the sea washed away the entire Reiderland. This is how the Dollard came into being.

In the middle of the night a man knocked at the door of the monastery Palmar, which was spared from the flood. A tall bowed figure asked for bread and shelter. Not for one night, but for good.

It was Tidde Winnenga, who had lost all he had.

There was room for him at the monastery, and they gave him food and lodging for as long as he lived.

This legend is known as folktale type SINSAG 1174, *Kleine Ursache, grosse Wirkung* (small cause, large consequence), and was collected by K. ter Laan in the province of Groningen. The translation is based on E. de Jong and P. Klaasse, *Sagen en Legenden van de Lage Landen* (Bussum, 1980), p. 54.

THE BASILISK OF UTRECHT

*I*n the basement of a tavern in Utrecht there lived a hideous monster that was hatched from a black rooster's egg by a snake.

The scientific name for such a dragon-snake was *basiliscus*. Since he only continues to live on in folktales and has not shown himself anywhere for ages, people presume that the species has died out now.

The glance of the *basiliscus* was so venomous that he could kill a man with a blink of the eye and pulverize him into a heap of dust.

Needless to say, the man who found the basilisk in the basement did not survive the adventure. He went down to fetch a barrel of beer. When he did not return, people thought that he had helped himself to the lager so generously that he was sleeping off his hangover. However, the next person who descended into the basement did not return either. When the impatient innkeeper stuck his head into the stairwell to ask what was keeping the men, he smelled a stench in the basement that convinced him something eerie was going on.

Just in time a monk, who was better acquainted with the supernatural than most of the ordinary guests in the barroom, managed to stop the innkeeper from investigating the matter.

The story of the monster in the basement spread through the town like wildfire and, to his despair, the innkeeper soon found that his clientele decreased.

He promised a large sum of money to the person who would rid him of the monster, but nobody dared to undertake such a precarious adventure.

Then one day a poorly dressed boy entered the tavern who dared to take the challenge. The only weapon that he carried was a plank, which he clenched against his body as a shield.

The innkeeper thought the boy was a halfwit and tried to stop him, but the boy seemed to be so self-assured that in the end he let him pass.

The boy descended the stairs with the plank against his chest. The monster waited for him in a corner of the subterranean vaulting. As soon as the boy was down in the basement, it crawled towards him. Its eyes spat fire and put the cellar all ablaze. Plumes of smoke rose from its nostrils and spread a horrible stench. The boy tried to hold his breath, and turned the plank around and kept it in front of him.

The backside was a mirror.

As soon as he aimed it in the direction of the basilisk, the monster was killed by its own image, and dropped down and was pulverized into a heap of dust.

This legend is known as folktale type SINSAG 1341, *Basilisk tötet Menschen durch seinen Blick (stirbt beim Sehen des eigenen Bildes im Spiegel)* (Basilisk kills people with a glance of his eyes; dies by seeing his own mirror image), and was collected by J. Cohen in the province of Utrecht. The translation is based on E. de Jong and P. Klaasse, *Sagen en Legenden van de Lage Landen* (Bussum, 1980), p. 143.

Part 7

CONTEMPORARY LEGENDS

DUTCH

*I*n the United States there still are orthodox Protestant communities whose ancestors came from the Netherlands. They are still trying to maintain the Dutch language, although it is not used for everyday purposes. The Bible they use is still in Dutch, though. The older adults in these communities regularly tell the same story about times past. There was an old lady in the United States who categorically refused to learn even a single word of English. She used the Dutch language exclusively, because, as she declared, "otherwise God won't be able to understand me."

This anecdote was told to me on October 31, 1995, by linguist Caroline Smits in Amsterdam (North Holland). I invented a new tale type for it: TM 4701, *God spreekt Nederlands* (God speaks Dutch). The translation is based on T. Meder, *De magische vlucht* (Amsterdam, 2000), p. 181.

THE POLICE ARE YOUR BEST FRIENDS

*O*ne Saturday, a man took a cycling tour through his own neighbourhood, and he could not help noticing a neat pile of tiles where a new house was being built. These tiles would come in handy, he thought, since he himself was busy tiling his kitchen. So he cycled home and returned with his car and a small trailer. However, while he was loading the tiles, a policeman approached.

"Allo, what do you think you're doing?"

"I've been tiling my kitchen and there were some tiles left. So when I saw this pile over here, I thought I could dump mine . . . ."

"No way," the policeman said, "everything back in again, and I'll stay here until the last tile is gone."

This urban legend is a version of what I call TM 6048, *Tegels Laden* (loading tiles). The story was told to collector Peter Burger on April 1, 1991, by Rinke Berkenbosch. The translation is based on Peter Burger, *De wraak van de kangoeroe* (Amsterdam, 1993), p. 69.

THE HITCHHIKER

*T*he following story was told in November 1991 in Hilversum.

Sometime in November, a man was driving on a motorway near Laren (like Hilversum, this is a place in the province of North Holland). He had invited a hitchhiker standing along the road to take a seat inside his car. Sitting beside the man, the hitchhiker struck up a conversation. The contents of this short talk can in no way be described as trivial. It was a monologue, in which the hitchhiker made an appeal to the man to reflect on some more spiritual values in life. In doing so, he reminded him of the upcoming feast of Christmas.

Very suddenly, any form of a tangible passenger could no longer be discerned in the car. Completely distressed, the man pulled over to the side of the road. Some police officers carrying out their road traffic surveillance duties urged him to drive on, and told him of having heard similar stories several times that afternoon.

The regional newspaper of Hilversum also carried a report of the "strange" events.

This urban legend is a version of BRUN 01000, *The Vanishing Hitchhiker*. The story was sent to the Meertens Institute in 1991 by a woman from Hilversum (North Holland) who wants to remain anonymous. The translation is based on T. Meder, *De magische vlucht* (Amsterdam, 2000), p. 166.

GRANDDAD ON THE RUN

*G*randdad went to Italy on holiday with his son and his family by caravan. On the way back, granddad died of a heart attack. In order to avoid a lot of problems, the family decided to leave immediately, hide the body in the caravan, and transport it across the borders illegally, so that the death could appear to have taken place in their own country. At the Swiss border, it appeared that the son had left his passport with the owner of the camping site. In order to gain time, the caravan was temporarily detached from the car while the family hastened back to the camping site. On their return to the border, the caravan (including the dead body) appeared to have been stolen. They never heard about it again . . . .

This urban legend is a version of BRUN 01100, *The Runaway Grandmother*. The story was sent to the Meertens Institute in 1991 by teacher Jan Naaijkens from Hilvarenbeek (North Brabant). The translation is based on T. Meder, *De magische vlucht* (Amsterdam, 2000), p. 167.

KANGAROO ROBS ATHLETE PARALYMPICS

*F*rom one of our reporters

ADELAIDE, Saturday

Yesterday, one of the Dutch contestants in the upcoming Paralympic Games was robbed by a kangaroo during training. It happened to cyclist Jan Mulder during a visit to a kangaroo park, where the team stayed as guests.

During this visit, a kangaroo bumped into the car of the Dutch team. The animal only suffered minor injuries.

Cyclist Jan Mulder took off the jacket of his tracksuit to take a photo. At the moment the photo was taken, the kangaroo took off with the jacket and the cyclist's Paralympic license.

This story is a version of BRUN 01120A, *The Kangaroo Thief* (*The Gucci Kangaroo*), and was published in the newspaper *De Telegraaf* on October 14, 2000. Later, Jan Mulder confessed that he had used the urban legend to attract the attention of journalists. Some three years later, this urban legend appeared in the American movie *Kangaroo Jack* (2003) as the major theme.

Although the action always takes place in Australia, the urban legend is well known in the Netherlands, too. In most versions, Dutch tourists bump into a kangaroo and put a jacket on him to take a funny picture. Then the kangaroo flees, taking along all the money, passports, and airplane tickets.

SMALL VERSUS BIG

*T*he following story was told in Amsterdam some ten years ago. It goes like this:

Along the canal, there was one open parking space. This parking space was approached from one side by a Citroen 2 CV (a "deux-chevaux") and by a big Mercedes Benz from the other side. The small 2 CV quickly turned into the parking space. The driver got out of the car and said, "This is the advantage of having a small car." The furious Merc driver pushed the 2 CV into the canal just like that and called out, "This is the advantage of having a big car!"

This urban legend is a version of BRUN 01215, *Old vs. Young*. The story was sent to the Meertens Institute on October 13, 1998, by E. Brandenburg from Grootebroek (North Holland). The translation is based on T. Meder, *De magische vlucht* (Amsterdam, 2000), p. 167.

IN CHAINS

*A*round closing time, the quiet frequenters of a disco were being threatened by a mob of excited, partly or fully intoxicated skinheads. One of the visitors just about managed to escape a guy who was chasing him with a chain. It was touch and go. When the man closed the door of his car in haste, the skinhead's chain hit the door and got stuck in it. The visitor rushed away at full speed. When he got home, he saw that the chain was connected to a ripped-off hand.

The story above was told as being true. Every time it was told, the storyteller had heard it from someone who knew someone who had heard it from someone (sometimes including this person's name), who had been there when it happened or who knew someone who was there at the time or knew the people it had happened to.

This urban legend is a version of BRUN 01405, *The Severed Fingers*. The story was sent to the Meertens Institute in 1991 by teacher Jan Naaijkens from Hilvarenbeek (North Brabant). The translation is based on T. Meder, *De magische vlucht* (Amsterdam, 2000), pp. 167–168.

THE TRUCK DRIVER

A truck driver stopped at a highway restaurant for a dinner.

Just after he got his order served, three Hell's Angels came in. They sat at the truck driver's table and tried to provoke him. One drank his coffee, the other took his fries, and the third ate his hamburger. The truck driver didn't speak a word, just stood up, paid, and left the restaurant.

One of the Hell's Angels said to the waitress, "What a wimp; he is too afraid to stick up for himself."

"Not only that," the waitress replied, "he is a lousy driver, too. He ran over three motorbikes just now!"

This tale can be told as a contemporary legend or as a joke. The story is a version of BRUN 01810, *Truckers and Bikers*. This (unpublished) tale was collected by Moniek Vis on December 19, 2001; she found it on the Dutch Internet site *Start De Dag Met Een Lach* (Start the Day with a Laugh).

ONCE A THIEF, ALWAYS A THIEF

*G*etting ready to leave their house in the morning, a couple discovered that their car had been stolen. They called the police to report the theft, and for the rest of the day they tried to manage without a car.

Imagine their surprise when they found their car in front of their house the next morning. There was a note on the dashboard, which read, "I want to apologize for the inconvenience I caused you, but I was desperately in need of a car! To make it up to you: here are two tickets for *La Traviata* this Friday. I wish you a pleasant evening."

The couple was pleasantly surprised and thought it rather amusing. They were not amused anymore, though, when they returned from the opera only to discover that their house had been skillfully stripped bare.

This urban legend is a version of BRUN 01835, *The Double Theft*. The translation is based on the publication Ethel Portnoy, *Broodje Aap,* 10th ed. (Amsterdam, 1992), p. 25.

THE SPOILT WEDDING

*I*n the province of Gelderland, a wedding was celebrated in a home. Pieces of pie were handed around and everybody took some. At a certain moment, granddad entered the kitchen and saw the cat gorging itself on some pie. He shooed the cat away and fumbled a bit with the pie so that the cat's nibblings could no longer be seen. He decided to keep silent about it.

One hour later, granddad went outside and saw the cat lying there. Dead.

Oh no, the pie was bad, granddad thought. He went back inside and felt obliged to tell the guests what had happened.

Panic all over. All the guests decided to go to hospital to have their stomachs pumped. And so it happened. The party was over.

That evening, the front door bell rang. The neighbour came in and asked:

"Did you find the cat?"

"Yes, why?" granddad asks.

"Well, I hit it with my car and I saw it was dead, but I thought, I'll tell them some other time, 'cause there was a wedding party going on here."

This urban legend is a version of BRUN 02110, *The Poisoned Pussycat at the Party*. The story was sent to the Meertens Institute in October 1998 by Mrs. E. C. W. Rutjes from Krommenie (North Holland). The translation is based on T. Meder, *De magische vlucht* (Amsterdam, 2000), pp. 170–171.

CHINESE FOOD

A married couple very fond of travelling had chosen China for their next destination. Their little dog, which was used to travelling with them wherever they went, was taken to a fancy restaurant on the first day after their arrival. The waiter approached and handed them the menu, but before they began studying it, the man first pointed at the dog and then at his open mouth, indicating that the dog should get some food, too. The waiter nodded understandingly, smiled amicably, and took the dog with him to the back of the restaurant.

"How nice," the couple said to each other. "Surely he'll be getting some food in the kitchen."

Meanwhile they had studied the menu, and although they had made their choice for quite a while, they waiter did not return to take their orders. Finally, after a long time, he approached the couple's table, holding a large dish with a cover on it.

"But we haven't ordered anything yet," they said, looking very surprised.

The cover of the dish was lifted. The woman screamed out loud and fainted at the sight of the dish. Amongst a deliciously fragrant meat dish lay the head of their little dog!

This urban legend is a version of BRUN 02300, *The Dog's Dinner*. The story was sent to the Meertens Institute on September 29, 1998, by Ingrid Stolwijk-Freichmann from De Kwakel (North Holland). The translation is based on T. Meder, *De magische vlucht* (Amsterdam, 2000), p. 168.

THE WANDERING COMFORTER

WINTERSWIJK (GPD)*—A couple from Winterswijk had the dubious honour of owning a wandering comforter. Directly after they bought it, they spread the comforter out over the bed, but after a while, to the amazement of the woman, she found the warm asset on the floor. In fact, the comforter took a hike more than once.

When it was returned to the interior decorating shop, the comforter revealed its mystery: The down inside had not been cleaned well enough and still contained pieces of skin. It was an ideal dwelling-place for a huge number of maggots, who were always in for a snack and therefore continuously kept the comforter in motion.

---

*Winterswijk is a town in the province of Gelderland. GPD stands for "Geassocieerde Pers Diensten" (Associated Press Agencies).

This story was published in the local newspaper *Leidsch Dagblad* on January 6, 1986 and was later exposed as an urban legend and published by Peter Burger in *De wraak van de kangoeroe* (Amsterdam, 1993), pp. 143–144, upon which this translation is based. It is supposed to be one of the few urban legends that has its narrative centre in the Low Countries. The tale is a version of BRUN 02415, *Contaminated Comforters*.

A DIRTY ROTTEN TRICK

For some decades now, people haven't wanted to swim in ordinary public swimming pools; they want to swim, play, and relax in a so-called subtropical swimming paradise. So several of these paradises have been built in the Netherlands. One of the main attractions is the waterslide: a pipe with curves inside and outside the building, ending up in a pool. In the late 1970s a brand new subtropical swimming paradise was to be opened. As an opening ritual, the young daughter of the mayor would come down the waterslide. Nobody knew that the night before some vandals had hammered several nails through the bottom of the waterslide, in a curve outside the building. Since no one had bothered to make a last inspection, the daughter of the mayor came down heavily mutilated, screaming and bleeding. At least, that's what I read in the local newspaper, in a short article titled "A dirty rotten trick." I agreed with that and was shocked for days. It took me some twenty years to realize that the journalist had fallen for an urban legend. As far as I know, the newspaper never retracted the story.

This tale is a version of BRUN 03270, *Razor Blades in Waterslide*. It is one of my own stories and has not been published before in this form. I can't remember the name of the newspaper, nor the name and location of the subtropical swimming pool.

THE FISHING TRIP

Taking a fishing boat to the Oosterschelde or the North Sea is a major tourist attraction in the Netherlands. Many people from the province of Zeeland and elsewhere retain good memories of such a day full of sea, wind, and sunshine.

*N*ot so long ago, a staff association hired a fishing boat for one day. At the crack of dawn, a group of men and women had gathered together at the landing stage, armed with fishing rods, bait, and other fishing gear. The weather conditions could have been better. Even though the sun was shining and the temperature was pleasant, one could feel a stiff breeze.

Still, this wasn't going to spoil the fun! High spirited, everyone embarked and off they went to the fishing grounds.

Once there, the wind blew much harder than they had expected. Actually, offshore it was really storming. Soon some of the wannabe fishermen started to have a rough time. Some of them had already become seasick when the boat reached its destination and the anchor was dropped. The people with sea legs attached the bait to their hooks and started fishing. It turned out to be a fine place for catching fish, and many showed that they were not afraid of a bit of sea wind. Soon the people with unsteady sea legs and upset stomachs discovered that one could better stand on deck and in the wind than stay down in the warm, stuffy saloon. That's why some of them, despite their misery, decided to cast a fishing line overboard.

Then it happened! While a fisherman was busy bringing in his catch, he suddenly had to "feed the fish," The worst part was that, along with the contents of his stomach, his false teeth vanished into the waves.

A few fellow anglers saw what had happened and immediately came up with a practical joke. In a corny mood because of the alcohol they had drunk, they persuaded another fisherman to take out his false teeth. Quickly, the dentures were tied to another fishing line and cast overboard.

All of a sudden, they yelled, "You're in luck today, Jan! Kees has caught your false teeth."

Full of disbelief, the unfortunate fisherman approached to take a look. It was true; there were indeed dentures dangling on the fishing line.

"You better try them," people suggested.

Jan put the false teeth into his mouth, but took them right out again and said, "They don't fit. Those aren't mine!" and he threw the dentures overboard instantly.

That's why that evening, two mumbling fishermen left the boat with toothless mouths, while the rest of their colleagues howled with laughter behind their backs.

This contemporary legend was told to one of the teachers accompanying a school student society fishing outing as being "true." It is well known in the Netherlands, and sometimes it is not told as being true, but as a joke. The international type is called BRUN 04155, *The Wrong Teeth*. The story was sent in by correspondent J. Boogaard (born 1933) from Goes (province of Zeeland), who used to be deputy headmaster of a junior secondary technical school. The story can be found in *Folklore Survey* 62 (1991): question # 3, form # I096 (archives Meertens Instituut, Amsterdam). The translation is based on T. Meder, *De magische vlucht* (Amsterdam, 2000), pp. 171–172.

THE MAN WHO LIKED BAKED BEANS

A man was very fond of baked beans all his life. He had one problem, though, they gave him such terrible wind. When he got married, he decided not to eat baked beans anymore, because he did not want his wife to suffer from the effects. For four years, he managed to stick to his decision. But one day he walked past a restaurant and smelled baked beans. He could not resist the temptation, went inside, and ate not one, not two, but three plates of baked beans. And then it began: pffrrt, pffrrt.

The man walked home: pffrrt, pffrrt. Before he rang the bell, he managed to squeeze out a big one: pppfffffrrrrrt. His wife opened the door and said, "Darling, I have a surprise for you. But I'll have to blindfold you first."

The man was blindfolded and put at the kitchen table by his wife.

"No peeking, mind," said his wife and she walked out of the kitchen.

Quickly, the man farted at length: pppfffrrrt!

And he waved the tails of his jacket about.

His wife returned and took off his blindfold. And what do you reckon?

There were twelve people sitting at the table!

This story was told in 1994 during a joke-telling contest on Dutch television called *Moppentoppers* (*Top Jokers*, broadcast by RTL4). The tale can be told as an urban legend as well, and is known as BRUN 05315, *The Fart in the Dark*. The translation is based on T. Meder, *De magische vlucht* (Amsterdam, 2000), p. 173.

GUARDIAN ANGEL

*T*his is a story about religious people, who could not find much relevant preaching regarding their particular faith in the area where they came from. As it happened, they had a friend in Switzerland, who invited them to a religious gathering.

With great anticipation, they went on their way. They were expected on Saturday night. But some fifteen miles outside Karlsruhe, they heard some strange ticking in their rear wheels. They pulled over on the shoulder, and it turned out that both the back wheel and the axle were very hot. Well, they took much care to drive to the first exit off the motorway, to get to a garage. It was Friday evening, and the garage was about to be closed. In the morning they would be the first to be attended to. Then it turned out that the rear bearing was broken (the car was a large Ford) and that the garage did not have a replacement bearing. They could get one in Karlsruhe, though. And since their last short drive had been fine, they were advised to drive slowly, and everything would probably be all right. They continued their journey, but the next garage was closed, too. The next advice they were given was to drive to Stuttgart; the garages are always open there. With a lot of praying and hoping, they went on their way again. Were they about to be faced with disappointment again?

The next garage could not offer any help either. What now? After another serious prayer, they decided to continue their journey. On the by-roads, mind you. This took a bit longer, but it struck them that the ticking sounds did not get worse anymore. In fact, they even became less prominent, or was that just their imagination? No, it was not. They regained courage. They did have to make a phone call to Beathenberg, for they were not supposed to arrive late. After some talking, things were settled. They would be allowed in on a Sunday morning just for this once.

They spent the night along the road, and arrived on Sunday morning at the time when the people were going into the assembly hall. They entered the hall as well, in their travel clothes. They were very grateful; God had heard their wishes and prayers.

On Monday, they drove to a garage. Once again, they wanted someone's professional opinion on the prospects of the car.

Some hours later, they went to collect the car. And guess what?

The garage owner said, "I've checked, cleaned and washed everything, but I cannot find as much as a scratch on the bearing."

All they had to pay for was the labour. They were sure of what had happened! The Lord God had seen their desire and fixed the car. Could it be true that, despite all, there was a guardian angel watching over them?

I like to call this tale type TM 6003, *Beschermengel biedt bijstand* (assistance from guardian angel). The story was sent to the Meertens Institute in 1991 by C. I. van der Weele from Gouda (South Holland). The translation is based on T. Meder, *De magische vlucht* (Amsterdam, 2000), pp. 176–177.

BICYCLE

*T*his was told as a true story. On the day that the oversized household refuse was collected in Alphen aan de Rijn, there was always a man on a carrier tricycle riding ahead of the dustcart to see if there was anything usable left on the pavement.

Around the same time, a postman had to deliver some letters in a block of flats. He parked his bicycle along the curb and entered the building. At that moment the man with the carrier tricycle arrived at the scene.

He took a look at the bicycle. What a ramshackle old thing, he thought to himself, but the wheels seemed usable enough. In a jiffy, he removed the wheels from the bike, put them on the luggage carrier of his tricycle, and rode off.

When the postman reappeared from the block of flats, he was shocked to see only the frame of his bike left at the curb. Lucky for him, there was a woman standing on the balcony in a block of flats nearby, who had seen everything. She called to the postman what had happened and gestured in which direction the man with the tricycle had gone.

The postman started running, and a few streets farther on, he overtook the man with the carrier tricycle. In high tones, he demanded his bicycle wheels back.

Soon after, the postman walked back to his bike with a wheel in each hand. Unfortunately the frame had in the meantime been collected by the garbage men.

I like to call this tale type TM 6011, *De fiets bij het vuilnis* (the bicycle at the garbage). The story was told on June 30, 1995, by Ben van der Have in Leiden (South Holland). The translation is based on T. Meder, *De magische vlucht* (Amsterdam, 2000), p. 177.

THE STOLEN CREDIT CARD

A friend of mine who lives in France these days told me a story that had happened to a friend of hers. This woman had one of those French credit cards with a withdrawal limit of 2,500 guilders, irrespective of one's balance. She kept this credit card in her purse in her bag. While shopping, she suddenly noticed the loss of her bag. She was in doubt whether her bag had been stolen or whether she left it behind somewhere by accident. However, she could not find the bag in any of the places she had been. Thinking of the high withdrawal limit on her credit card, she immediately made a phone call to freeze her account. In the meantime, no money had disappeared from her account. Furthermore, she reported the loss of her bag and its contents. At the end of that same afternoon, the police phoned her back: Her bag had been recovered. Most of her possessions were still in it. Even her purse was still in the bag, but the money and the credit card had been removed from it. The woman was told she could collect the bag and its contents at the police station the following morning at 9 a.m.

The following morning the woman went to the police station in question, at the other end of town. The policemen knew nothing about a retrieved bag or indeed, a phone call. When the woman returned home, she found her entire house ransacked. The phone call had not come from the police, but from the thieves, who had seized their chance and made good use of her absence.

This contemporary legend belongs to the folktale type TM 6036, *De gestolen creditcard* (the stolen credit card). The story was told to me on January 2, 1995, by Ineke Lodder-Kooij in Schiedam (South Holland). The translation is based on T. Meder, *De magische vlucht* (Amsterdam, 2000), pp. 189–190.

COLD AS ICE

The storyteller heard this story in the supermarket where she and her husband both work. People were pretending it was a true story.

During a hot summer, a man became unwell at the checkout. He started perspiring heavily and fell to the floor, having lost consciousness. The store employees phoned an ambulance, and guess what? The male nurse took the man's hat off and saw a frozen chicken hidden under it. The reason he has become unwell was that it was so hot and he had hidden the ice cold product on his head. It was not sweat, but water from the chicken thawing out that dripped down his face.

There are other versions of this story, involving stolen fish fingers or a woman trying to perform this theft with steak, so that she even had blood running from under her hat and down her face.

This urban legend is a version of BRUN 06215, *The Shoplifter and the Frozen Chicken.* The story was sent to the Meertens Institute on October 21, 1998, by Debby Moonen from Sittard (Limburg). The translation is based on T. Meder, *De magische vlucht* (Amsterdam, 2000), p. 178.

THE INSOLUBLE SUM

*T*he storyteller heard that in the school for lower general secondary education (in Dutch, *Mavo*) that a friend of his attended, a new teacher had been appointed just before the final exams. For the physics exam, he wrote down two sums. He said the one on the left could not be solved, whereas the one on the right could. A boy came in very late, so he didn't hear about one of the sums being insoluble. He managed to solve both of them, even within the set time. The storyteller doesn't know if it's true, but it sounded like a nice story. Later he saw the same idea in the movie *Good Will Hunting*. For that reason, he found it even funnier.

This urban legend is a version of BRUN 10200, *The Unsolvable Math Problem*. The story was told to collector Elise de Bree on September 5, 1998, by Laurens Calon from Goirle (province of North Brabant). The translation is based on T. Meder, *De magische vlucht* (Amsterdam, 2000), pp. 188–189.

WHAT IS "GUTS"?

$\mathcal{D}$uring exams, one of the assignments for Dutch was, "Write an essay on the subject 'What is guts?' " Someone turned in three empty sheets of paper, and at the bottom of the last page he had written, "This is guts." An old friend of the storyteller claimed she knew someone who had actually done this.

This contemporary legend belongs to the folktale type BRUN 10235, *"Define 'Courage'."* The story was told on June 25, 1998, to Wendy de Visser by Stefanie Wels from Amsterdam (North Holland). The translation is based on T. Meder, *De magische vlucht* (Amsterdam, 2000), p. 189.

CIRCUS BEAR

"*D*id you read that article in the paper, about that bear hunt in Romania? No? Well, it was about a German guy who was staying in one of those guest houses in Romania. He told the landlord he loved to hunt. The landlord wanted to boast a little and said that there were many bears in the environs. The German quite fancied the idea of a bear hunt, so he said he would return some day with a couple of friends to do some hunting. The landlord had completely forgotten about it, when some time later, a group of six or so Germans turned up on his doorstep with shotguns. Now it was too late for the landlord to say there weren't actually any bears in the area. So he went to the village to seek some advice. He was told that there was someone in the area who kept an old circus bear. So they concocted a plan to give this circus bear its freedom. If it was shot that would be a pity, but it was an old animal after all. Should the Germans miss, then that wouldn't be too bad either. So some time later, those Germans were lying next to a road with their shotguns. A Romanian cycled by and saw a bear a bit farther on. The shock caused the man to jump from his bike and run like hell. A few moments later, the German hunters saw a bear cycling past. After all, it was a circus bear. The Germans did not shoot, but went back home instead. I can imagine their faces. It was in the Dutch newspaper *de Volkskrant*. When you read the beginning of such a story, you are willing to believe it, but at the end, when that bear comes cycling past . . . ."

This story was told to me by Herman Beekveldt in Amsterdam, on November 29, 1996. There is no international folktale type available. The translation is based on T. Meder, *De magische vlucht* (Amsterdam, 2000), pp. 192–193.

BIOLOGY PRACTICAL

A girl is a freshman and has a biology practical in which she has to study dead skin cells under a microscope. As usual the tutor tells her to scratch along the inside of her cheek with her nail or with a spatula a few times in order to get the necessary skin cells. Then she has to place the collected material on a slide, put a piece of plastic on it, and put it under the microscope to examine it. The girl does all this and sees something moving in the sample. She doesn't know what it is, and asks the tutor whether he does. The tutor looks at her sample through the microscope and says it isn't very important. The girl, however, is determined to know what it is and urges the tutor to tell her. The tutor refuses several times, and by the time he is finally prepared to tell her, the attention of the other students has of course been attracted. Eventually, the tutor says that the moving bits are male sperm cells, whereupon the girl blushes heavily; she had had oral sex with a boy that morning.

The story was sent via e-mail to the Meertens Institute by Willem Ladiges from Amsterdam (North Holland) on November 6, 1998. There is no international folktale type available. The translation is based on T. Meder, *De magische vlucht* (Amsterdam, 2000), p. 193.

FISHING IN THE MIST

"On a misty morning, I went out fishing.

The mist was so thick, I could park my bike against it. I cast my fishing line, but of course, I could not see the float. I felt I had something, hauled in my line, and what do you reckon? The bait was on the hook, entirely flat. I just didn't understand it. After a while, when the mist became thinner, it became clear to me. I wasn't fishing along the canal, but along a cycle path, and a bike had flattened my bait."

This story was sent in in 1991 by Mrs. L. H. Jeurink-Hofsteenge, a saleswoman from Emmen (province of Drente); she heard the tale from her father-in-law, who had told it as a true story. There is no international folktale type available. The translation is based on T. Meder, *De magische vlucht* (Amsterdam, 2000), p. 196.

SHARP FOOD

A young man went to visit his fiancée and her mother in Amsterdam and brought along a box of thin, square chocolates with a filling of soft mint.* His fiancée and her mother both took one. Inside the fiancée's chocolate a razor blade was found. After the police had been informed, they interrogated the young man sharply. Since he kept maintaining his innocence, the police turned to the manufacturer, who demonstrated that nowhere in the production process could a razor blade possibly wind up in a chocolate. So the police are still hunting for a maniac who puts razor blades in chocolates.

---

*The candy called "After Eights."

The translation is based on Ethel Portnoy, *Broodje Aap*. 10th ed. (Amsterdam, 1992), p. 103. There is no international folktale type available.

TRIVIAL

*D*uring a formal lecture, a university professor mentioned a certain detail and remarked, "I am not going into that any further, because it's trivial." Then the professor, sunk deep in thought, left the classroom, returned half an hour later, and remarked, "I have looked it up, and it appears to be trivial indeed," and without further ado continued his lecture.

This absent-minded professor legend was sent to me on November 30, 1995, by e-mail; the storyteller was Freek Wiedijk from Utrecht. The translation is based on T. Meder, *De magische vlucht* (Amsterdam, 2000), pp. 193–194.

Part 8

RIDDLES AND PUZZLES

THE WOLF, THE GOAT, AND THE CABBAGE

*O*ne day, there was a man who arrived at a stream with a goat, a cabbage, and a wolf. There was a small boat with which he could row his load to the other side. However, he could only carry one thing at a time. What did he have to do?

If he were to bring the cabbage to the other side first, the wolf would eat the goat.

If he brought the wolf to the other side first, the goat would eat the cabbage.

So first of all, he brought the goat to the opposite side. The cabbage would be safe with the wolf, who had no taste for cabbages.

Then the man brought the cabbage to the other side. However, he put the goat in the boat again and rowed back, because the goat was not to be trusted alone with the cabbage.

Next, the goat went out of the boat, while the wolf went in and was brought to the other side.

After that, the man went back to bring the goat to the opposite side again. So the goat made three trips altogether.

This riddle is internationally known as folktale type ATU 1579, *Carrying Wolf, Goat, and Cabbage across Stream*. It was told on September 16, 1974, in the Frisian language to collector A. A. Jaarsma by the working-class storyteller Bonne Dijkstra, who lived in Molenend (Friesland). His version of the riddle has not been published before, and the translation is based on the Jaarsma Collection, report 1145, tale no. 18 (archive and Dutch Folktale Database, Meertens Instituut, Amsterdam).

THE TWO GUARDS

*Y*ou are sitting in a prison cell. In your cell there are two doors. Behind one door there is a pit full of crocodiles. Behind the other door there is a way out. There is a guard standing in front of each door. One guard always speaks the truth, the other always lies, but you don't know which one does which. You are allowed to leave your cell, and you are allowed to ask one guard one question. Which question should you ask to find the door to freedom for sure?

Solution: You must ask one guard: "What door will the other guard say leads to freedom?" Since there will always be a lie involved, you should choose the other door than the one mentioned, and you will be free.

This internationally known riddle was told to me on June 22, 2003, by Mrs. Micky Marsman in Epe (Gelderland). The translation is based on an unpublished fieldwork report (archive and Dutch Folktale Database, Meertens Instituut, Amsterdam).

THE SNAIL IN THE PIT

A pit is twenty metres deep and completely empty. At the bottom of the pit is a snail. By day, the snail manages to climb up five metres. By night, however, he slides down four metres again. So in a twenty-four-hour period, he actually climbs one metre. How many days will it take the snail to climb out of the pit?

Solution: It will take the snail sixteen days. After climbing for fifteen days, he will have reached the level of fifteen metres. In the daytime next day, he will climb the remaining five metres; he won't slide down anymore, because now he has already left the pit.

This riddle was told to me on January 9, 2000, by the young Moroccan storyteller Mohamed Remadan in Utrecht (Utrecht). The translation is based on Theo Meder and Marie van Dijk, *Doe open Zimzim* (Amsterdam, 2000), p. 61.

THE ROOM WITH THREE LIGHTBULBS

*T*here is a hallway, and on both sides of the hallway there is a door. Behind each door is a room. Both rooms are completely empty. In the one room there are just three lightbulbs hanging from the ceiling. They are not burning. In the other room, there are three switches. Only one switch will turn on a lightbulb in the other room, but you don't know which switch. You are allowed to turn on as many switches as you like, but you may only go once and have a look in the other room to find out if there is a lightbulb burning. How can you be absolutely sure which switch turns on the only connected lightbulb?

Solution: Turn on the first switch and do nothing; just wait for half an hour. Then turn the first switch off and turn the second one on. Now you walk to the other room. If there is a lightbulb burning, that's because of the second switch. If there is no lightbulb burning, go and feel the lightbulbs. If one lightbulb is warm, that is because of the first switch you had turned on. If all the lightbulbs are cold, you know for sure that the third switch will turn on a lightbulb.

This riddle was told to me on January 9, 2000, by the young Moroccan storyteller Mohamed Remadan in Utrecht (Utrecht). The translation is based on Theo Meder and Marie van Dijk, *Doe open Zimzim* (Amsterdam, 2000), pp. 61–63.

RIDDLE-JOKES

Who invented copper wire?

Two Dutchmen fighting over a cent.

What does a Dutchman do if he offers you refreshment?

He opens a window.

How do the Dutch police stop a demonstration?

By shaking collection-boxes.

What's the most beautiful place in Friesland?

The bus stop to Groningen.*

What's yellow and goes back in time?

The bus to Limburg.

What do you call Limburgians?

Spare-Belgians.

What happens if a Limburgian moves to Belgium?

The IQ rate rises on both sides of the border.

Why does a Belgian have scratches on his face on Monday?

Because during the weekend he tried to eat with a knife and fork again.

Why does a Belgian take hay to bed?

To feed the nightmare.

What do you do if a Belgian throws a hand grenade at you?

Just pull the pin and throw it back.

How can you keep a Belgian busy for a long time?

Give him a piece of paper with "please turn over" written on both sides.

Why does a Belgian have a knife in his car?

To cut corners.

Why does a Belgian have empty bottles of beer in the refrigerator?

For the people who don't want to drink.

How can you make a Belgian crazy?

By putting him in a round room and telling him there is a bag of fries** in the corner.

What strikes you if you compare a Belgian with a cow?

The intelligent look in the eyes of the cow.

Why does a German have to be buried with his mouth closed?

To save a lot of sand.***

What's the thinnest book ever written called?

"Five centuries of German humour."

How do Germans open a mussel?

They knock on it very loudly and shout: "Aufmachen!"****

What's the difference between men and pigs?

Pigs don't turn into men after they drink alcohol.

Why are men, men and rats, rats?

The rats got to choose first.

What's the penalty for bigamy?

Two mothers-in-law.

What does a dumb blonde say if she picks up her mobile phone?

"How did you know I was here?"

What's blonde and smart?

A golden retriever.

What does a dumb blonde think if she sees a banana peel lying on the sidewalk?

"Oh no, there I go again . . . ."

What happens when a dumb blonde swallows a fly?

She'll have more brains in her stomach than in her head.

Why do women have four brain cells?

One for each stove burner.

How do you open a champagne factory?

By throwing a ship against it.

What do you call a boomerang that doesn't return?

A stick.

It's green and if you throw it against the wall, the phone starts ringing at your neighbour's. What's that?

Coincidence, pure coincidence.

Why does a gnome wear wooden shoes?*****

So he won't be detected floating upside down in a bowl of custard.

What do you get if you cross an elephant with a mole?

Very large holes in your backyard.

He walks through the desert and talks all day. Guess who?

Ali Blabla.

What do you call a dog without legs?

It doesn't matter what you call him; he won't come anyway.

Why do government officials never go on strike?

No one would notice.

What has two eyes and sixty-four teeth?

A crocodile.

What has sixty-four eyes and two teeth?

A busload of old-age pensioners.

How can you throw an egg against the wall without breaking it?

By leaving the chicken around it.

It's yellow, and if it hits you in the eye, you are dead. What is it?

A train.

Why is a fire engine red?

The fire department uses hoses.

In hoses there is water.

Fish live in the water too.

Fish have fins.

The Finns live next to the Russians.

The Russians used to have a red flag.

That's why fire engines are red.

What's sitting in a tree and hissing?

A nest of young bicycle pumps.

It's white and running across the desert. What's that?

A herd of yoghurt.

What's the difference between a crocodile?******

The more he greens, the more he swims.

What's the difference between a dead bird?

One leg is shorter than the other.

---

*Friesland and Groningen are competing provinces in northeast Netherlands.

**According to the stereotype, Belgians are notorious for eating (French) fries.

***According to the stereotype, Germans have big mouths.

****"Open up!" This riddle refers to German practices during World War II.

*****Custard and traditional wooden shoes are both yellow.

******The last two riddles are extra absurd, because not only the answer but also the question is ridiculous.

These (unpublished) jokes in the form of riddles are a selection taken from the Dutch Folktale Database and were collected between 1994 and 2005.

Part 9

ANECDOTES AND JOKES

THE GIFT OF THE GHOST

A man with a hump and a man with a wooden leg are sitting in a pub together. Near closing time, the man with the hump wants to go home, but the man with the wooden leg decides to stay and have one for the road.

The man with the hump leaves and takes the shortest way home, through the graveyard. When he walks across the graveyard, a ghost suddenly walks up to him and calls out, "Wooo, wooo, what's that on your back?"

"Oh, it's a hump," the man says, resigned.

"Give it to me," the ghost says and takes the hump away.

The next evening, the man tells his friend in the pub what has happened to him: "I'm walking through the graveyard, right? And then this ghost walks up to me, asks me what I've got on my back and takes my hump away, just like that! You know what you should do? You should walk across the graveyard tonight too!"

That same evening, the man with the wooden leg walks across the graveyard. Then all of a sudden, the ghost appears, calling out, "Wooo, wooo, what's that on your back?"

"Well . . . . . Nothing!"

Then the ghost says, "Here's a hump for you!"

This joke was told to me in the 1970s by Cor Hersbach in 's-Gravenzande (South Holland). It is a humorous version of ATU 503, *The Gifts of the Little People*. The translation is based on T. Meder, *De magische vlucht* (Amsterdam, 2000), p. 207.

THE SNOW-CHILD

A captain came home after a sea voyage of some four or five years. At home, he found his family extended with a little son, so instead of four children he now had five.

The captain asked his wife where this son came from, and she answered, "Well, my dear husband, it seems to be some kind of divine intervention. About two years ago I was taking a walk in the forest, thinking about you, and a snowflake fell into my lap. On that day I became pregnant, and I gave birth to this son."

The captain swallowed the story. A few years later he went on a long journey again, and took his son along, but returned home without him.

Immediately, his wife asked where her son was, whereupon the captain answered, "Well, my dear wife, it seems to have been some kind of intervention indeed, and it is now confirmed that the boy was made of snow, for when we passed the equator, he melted at once."

This version of ATU 1362, *The Snow-Child*, was collected by G. J. Boekenoogen, found in a small jest book dating from 1859 called *Knollen en Citroenen*. An even older Dutch version has been found in a jest book from 1554 called *Een nyeuwe clucht Boeck*. The translation is based on T. Meder and C. Hendriks, *Vertelcultuur in Nederland* (Amsterdam, 2005), p. 471.

WHO'S IN CHARGE?

*O*nce upon a time there was a gentleman whose wife always wanted to be in charge of things. He told her that women always wanted to have the last word, which she subsequently denied.

Then the gentleman said, "I will prove I'm right."

He called his stable hand and asked to do him a favour.

"Take along a basket of apples and three horses: a white one, a black one, and a grey one. Go along the houses and ask people who's the boss there. If the woman is in charge, you give them two apples. If the man is in charge, he may choose one of the horses."

The stable hand went on his way, but everywhere he went, the wife appeared to be in charge, so he had to give away more and more apples.

Then he arrived at a farm where the man seemed to be grumpy and hot-tempered.

"Who is in charge over here?" the stable hand asked.

"I am," the farmer replied.

"Well," the stable hand said, "that's something else for a change. Please, follow me. From these three horses you may pick out one. You may decide for yourself."

The farmer chose the black horse and called it a splendid creature. Then his wife came along.

"Look, I chose the black one," the farmer said, "that's the most beautiful one."

"Oh dear, no," his wife said, "not the black one. The grey one is much more beautiful."

"No way!" the farmer replied, "these grey ones turn pale so soon."

Still, the farmer's wife insisted.

"I say, take the grey one," she said.

Finally, the farmer said to her, "Well, you decide then."

"The grey one," she said.

"The grey one," the farmer repeated to the stable hand.

"You can't have it," the stable hand said to him. "You told me that you were in charge, but now I hear quite differently."

To the farmer's wife he said, "You are the boss."

"Yes," she agreed.

"I give you two apples."

The stable hand came home with three horses, but the basket of apples was completely empty.

So the gentleman was absolutely right!

This version of ATU 1375, *Who Can Rule His Wife?*, was told in Nijega (Friesland) by Mrs. Geeske Kobus-Van der Zee on June 15, 1966, and was recorded by collector A. A. Jaarsma. The translation from Frisian is based on T. Meder, *De magische vlucht* (Amsterdam, 2000), pp. 207–208.

WHOSO DIGGETH A PIT . . .

*O*nce upon a time, there were a man and a woman who were very rich. The woman, however, was greedy enough to try and get it all for herself. So she told a neighbour, and her neighbour gave her some advice: "Give him four eggs and a jug of milk every morning. Then he'll go blind eventually and drown himself."

So she did, and after three months, she became ill herself.

"Well, my dear lady wife," said her husband, "because you've been so good to me, I want to do the same for you."

So he went over to his neighbour and asked her for advice. She told the man what a trick she had been playing on his wife. When the woman was better, she went to see her neighbour and said that her husband wouldn't go blind.

"Well," said the woman, "in that case give him four eggs and two jugs of milk."

So she did, and after a while, he started to complain that he was blind, although he could see very well.

Aha, the woman thought, it's beginning to work.

A few days later, the man said, "Oh wife, I am going to drown myself. Would you be kind enough to escort me to the lake?"

She was happy to do so.

When they arrived at the lake, the man said, "Sweet wife, will you give me a push, so that I will fall in?"

The woman took a few steps back, walked towards her husband with some speed, and . . . her husband jumped aside, and because she couldn't slow down enough in time, she fell in herself.

"Help, help," the wife cried.

"Oh wife, it's no use. After all, I can't see anything," said her husband and returned home.

This tale is a version of AT 1380, *The Faithless Wife.* The joke was sent to collector G. J. Boekenoogen in February 1894 by thirteen-year-old Jacobes Andereas Bruning from Den Helder (North Holland). The translation is based on T. Meder, *De magische vlucht* (Amsterdam, 2000), p. 238.

THE BLIND SPINSTER

*O*nce upon a time there was a young woman who was almost blind. For this reason, it was practically impossible for her to get any sweethearts.

Every day she got water from the well. Her neighbour was a widower, who had recently moved to the area. He saw her there at the well every day.

"You're always pretty busy," he said. "I would like to have you as my housekeeper."

"I don't want to come to you as a housekeeper," she said, and ran off fast.

She lived with her mother, who was a widow. On Sunday evening, the floor was neatly swept with sand. When everything was neat and tidy, there was somebody at the door. It was their neighbour. He came to see the daughter. They got talking and went for a walk later that evening.

They agreed he would come around again the next Sunday evening.

Then her mother put a tiny needle on the floor and the daughter memorized its exact spot.

At a certain moment, when her lover had been around for a while, she suddenly said, "I say, Barend, is that a needle over there?"

She picked up the needle, and Barend mentioned that the people from the village said that her eyesight wasn't all that good. He now understood, however, that this was mere gossip.

It was agreed that Barend would come round again the next Sunday evening.

But that evening, things went wrong. When they returned from their walk, the coffee-pot was on the table. But she mistook it for the cat and said, "Shoo Puss!" And immediately she knocked the entire pot full of piping hot coffee off the table.

Barend knew enough now. He never returned there. Years later the young woman ended up in a mental home. By that time, she couldn't see anything anymore. It was there that she told her story.

The tale is a version of ATU 1456, *The Blind Fiancée*. This story was told on March 16, 1966, to collector A. A. Jaarsma by Mrs. Geeske Kobus-Van der Zee from Nijega (Friesland). The translation from Frisian is based on T. Meder, *De magische vlucht* (Amsterdam, 2000), p. 209.

THE MASTER THIEF

*O*nce upon a time, there was a father who had one son. He had had his son learn everything that could possibly be learned.

One day the father said, "Listen, my boy. What would you like to do now? You are my only child and heir. I am immensely rich. You have learned everything. Now tell me what you would like to do."

"Father," the son said, " 'tis true, I learned many a thing, but not everything. I have never learned to rob and steal, which I would like to learn as well."

The father was shocked enormously and said, "But my dear boy, what is this supposed to mean? Robbing and stealing? But you're incredibly rich!"

"This may be true," said the son, "but father, these treasures could be taken away from either you or me, and if I am able to rob and steal, I could make a living that way too, if everything else is of no avail."

The father wept and lamented intensely about his child's incomprehensible wish, but no matter how he prayed, threatened, or begged, his son wanted to learn about robbing and stealing. When the father realized that he couldn't change his son's decision, he went to see the leader of a band of robbers and came to an understanding with him to take on his son as an apprentice. The conclusion of this conversation was that the son would be accepted among the robbers for the duration of one year, but that he, like all apprentices, would be obliged to prove his competence before he left. And it was no sooner said than done.

The son joined the robbers, stole and learned as much as he could, and when the year was almost over, he reminded the leader of his departure.

"Very well," said the leader. "You can leave, but you know the conditions."

"Well," said the son, "why don't you give me a test?"

"Listen to this," said the leader. "A farmer will pass through the forest, sitting on a horse, and behind the horse, there will be a sheep with a little bell under its throat. The sheep will be tied to the horse's tail. Your task is to steal the sheep, as well as the horse, and to put the farmer in a well, naked. And you will have to do this all on your own."

The son promised to perform this task to prove his competence.

Thus his labour began. He climbed a tree, and after having waited patiently for several hours, he heard the farmer coming on his horse, and the sheep right behind him. In the distance, he could hear the sound of the little bell. He now descended from the tree and hid behind it. When the farmer had passed, he followed him silently, widened the loop around the sheep's neck, pulled it over its head, and left the loop and the bell hanging behind the horse. Then he took the sheep to a place known to him. Since he knew his way around the woods better than the farmer, he took a side road and consequently ended up at a spot on the main road the farmer still had to pass.

The farmer, who had walked on for a while without getting suspicious (after all, he kept hearing the little bell), happened to take a look behind him and o dear! he missed his sheep. He checked the loop and noticed that it had been pulled over the head of the sheep.

That poor animal, he thought, I will go and look for it, otherwise it will surely lose its way in the forest. In order to be able to have a good look around in the undergrowth as well, the farmer went on foot, and tied his horse to a tree for the time being. He had absolutely no idea that the sheep had been stolen. When he was thus looking for his sheep, the robbers' apprentice appeared. He cut loose the horse, took it to his place of safety, and then sat near a well in the forest, crying out loud.

The farmer, who couldn't find his sheep no matter how he kept looking, returned in disappointment to the place where he had left his horse. But imagine his shock when, returned to the spot, he found his horse was gone! This left him no choice but to think he had been robbed. That poor farmer, how sad he was. While he was thinking about the fastest way to get out of the forest, before it became dark, he heard very loud noises and crying, not too far away from him. Following the crying sounds, he arrived at the well where the robbers' apprentice was sitting, and asked him what the matter was.

"Ah, good man," the robbers' apprentice said, "I am a merchant of gold and gems. When I was passing through the forest, I was held up by robbers, who took my valuables away from me. Now I've become a poor man."

"Well, you poor wretch," said the farmer, "that makes us partners in adversity, for oh, I don't know what to do either! Surely 'twas those same robbers who stole my horse and sheep."

And the farmer joined in the moaning.

"Hush, man," said the robbers' apprentice. "I'll tell you something. Be quiet about your loss. Do you see that black spot over there in that well? Well, that is the most valuable case of all, containing my jewels. The robbers had quite a load already, and they thought this was only a case containing silver. So for the time being, they threw it into the well and planned to get it later."

"Well," said the farmer, "why don't you get it out, so you'll have your treasure back after all?"

"Oh, dear, good man," the apprentice said, "can't you see that I'm half-dead with fear and woe? No, I'd rather have you get it out. I promise you, you'll have two horses and a sheep from me in return."

Well, the farmer quite liked the idea.

"But how will I get into the well? And I will become ever so wet."

"I know what to do," said the apprentice. "Strip naked, sit on that bucket, and I'll let you down. As soon as you have the case, you can call me, I'll pull you back up, and you can get dressed again. Then you'll be dry, and I will give you your reward."

And it was no sooner said than done. The farmer sat naked on the bucket, the robber let him down, and when the farmer called out, "I can't feel any case down here!" the apprentice replied, "You can say that again, my friend! Just you stay down there for a while."

Heavens above, how terrified this farmer was! But the robbers' apprentice laughed up his sleeve, went to see his mates, and told them about the successful conclusion of his assignment. Now all the robbers, including the leader and the apprentice, went to the forest, dressed as gentlemen. There they found the sheep and the horse, and, having arrived at the well, they saw the farmer sitting in the well, totally naked. The cold and the fear of facing death down there in that well had rendered him virtually speechless. The gentlemen robbers pulled him up and asked him how he, stripped and all, had ended up in that well. After having recovered himself, the poor farmer told them what had happened to him.

When he had told them everything, the leader said, "After all, you're actually a stupid farmer, 'cause who would crawl naked into a well for some stranger? Would you recognize this guy? Have a look around and see if he's among this group of gentlemen."

"O no, noble lord," said the farmer, "I wouldn't even dare thinking that. He was definitely no gentleman, but a nasty robber, dressed as a merchant."

"Well," the leader said, "this guy promised you two horses and a sheep. Here is a purse full of money, which will buy you your promised reward—you're allowed something for your fear. . . . . And now begone with you."

Then the leader turned to the son and said, "You've shown yourself a man of the trade. Your test was completed utterly successfully. With this laudation as your diploma, you can leave, although it pains us to see you go. If ever there are difficult times for you, we will welcome you back to our guild with open arms."

And thus the son returned to his father.

The tale is a version of ATU 1525, *The Master Thief.* The story was sent to collector G. J. Boekenoogen in 1894 by Mrs. Deenik from Haarlem (North Holland). The translation is based on T. Meder and C. Hendriks, *Vertelcultuur in Nederland* (Amsterdam, 2005), pp. 126–128.

THE SHEEPHEADS OF DORDRECHT

*I*n the old days, when an inhabitant of Dordrecht wished to import meat from outside the city, he had to pay a tax. However, most people tried every trick in the book to avoid this.

One morning a father said to his son, "Tomorrow, I would like to eat a nice leg of mutton."

To which the boy replied, "Father, at these words my heart rejoices, and so does my stomach!"

"Still, I refuse to make the city any richer than it is already. We are going to smuggle!"

"To smuggle? While the collector of taxes is standing at the city gate?!"

"Even if there are thirty collectors of taxes standing at the gate, we will get that sheep past them."

The father whispered something in the boy's ears, whose mouth opened wider and wider in amazement. "But father . . . ."

"Let's go right away!"

In the rural surroundings of the city they searched for the fattest sheep around, and they squeezed the backs of many bleating animals before they made their choice. Finally they found a bloated sheep, and after they had bought it, they looked at each other and their eyes twinkled with delight. Water was running from their mouths and over their coats.

"Boiled with onions!" the father said.

"Roasted!"

"Broiled on the spit."

"O, stop now, cut it out!"

As soon as they were alone in the field, the son fetched a package that he had carried along all day.

"Ha ha ha ha!" the man laughed, "now let's fool the tax collector."

In the meantime, the boy was dressing the animal in boy's clothes and finally pulled a hat over its ears and eyes. It had started to grow dark already. Some clouds turned black against the sky, and on the horizon the night started unfolding its shadowy wings.

The man and the boy pulled the sheep upright, each with a front leg under his arm. They started walking with the sheep between them, while the animal stumbled along—as best it could—on its hind legs. It looked like they were pulling along an extremely tired little brother. No wonder "he" had become tired, for "he" was such a fat boy . . . .

Slowly they approached the gate. The collector of taxes saw them coming, nodded, and started a conversation.

"Nice weather, ain't it?"

They had to stand still now.

"Yes, splendid."

"The boy is tired, obviously," the tax collector remarked.

"He's exhausted!"

"Little brother shouldn't eat so much. He's way too fat."

"Baaaaa!" little brother exclaimed, and they were caught red-handed.

Soon it was widely known that inhabitants of Dordrecht had in vain attempted to smuggle a sheep in boy's clothes into the city. It did not take long before people from surrounding cities gave the inhabitants of Dordrecht the nickname sheepheads.

This legend is a version of the international folktale type ATU 1624B*, *The Theft of Bacon*. Actually, an older nickname for the people of Dordrecht (South Holland) was Sheep's Thieves. Perhaps in older versions of the tale the sheep was not bought but stolen. In 1919 the collector Josef Cohen made the people from Dordrecht a little less criminal by turning them into clumsy sheep smugglers and calling them sheepheads, which in Dutch means simpletons. This slightly reworked translation is based on R. A. Koman, *Bèèh . . . ! Groot Dordts volksverhalenboek* (Bedum, 2005), p. 22.

JAN WITH THE MAGIC POT

*O*nce upon a time there was a man who could not afford the rent for his house.

The landlord said, "Listen to me, Jan, if you cannot pay the rent, you'll have to get out."

"Oh well," Jan said to his wife, "in that case I suppose we'll have to slaughter our only cow. That'll give us something to eat and we can sell the skin, which will cover at least a part of our rent."

He went to the market with the skin. He stood there in the rain and the wind for over three hours, but nobody came to have a look at the skin. Evening was beginning to fall and he did not have a clue what to do next. Close to where he stood were the windows of the town hall. The light was on in one of the rooms, and the gentlemen of the town hall were counting a large sum of money.

Jan thought, I wish I had that money.

He did not waste too much time thinking about it, crawled inside the animal skin, and rushed up the stairs of the town hall, roaring and stamping. He gave the gentlemen a right start. They fled and left their money and all behind. Jan quickly crawled out of the skin and filled it with money, which he took home with him.

"Wife," he said, "go to our neighbour to lend his potato measure, for I want to measure the money with it."

The wife got the measure and Jan measured four gallons of money in small change, dimes and quarters. The next day he went to pay the landlord.

"Well, Jan," said the landlord, "where did you get all this money?"

"Well, sir, I slaughtered one of my animals, and skins are expensive on the market."

"Really?"

"Yes, I got four gallons of money for it."

"Well," said the landlord, "in that case I will also sell two animal skins on the market."

And he sent his servant to the market with the skins of his two best milk cows. While the servant was standing at the market with the skins, a Jew came by to ask how much he wanted for them.

"Four gallons," he told the Jew.

"Oh dear, me and my entire family don't have as much as four gallons of money."

So the servant returned home with the skins.

"No sale?"

"No, sir, they were not even prepared to offer as much as ten guilders. The Jew made an offer of two guilders."

Then the landlord went to see Jan, but Jan had seen him coming and said to his wife, "You should do some complaining to me, and tell me that I'm bad, and then I will stab you to death; wait, let me hide the guts with blood under your clothes, so I can stick my knife into that."

"By God, Jan," said the landlord, "what a liar you are! Imagine deceiving someone like that!"

"Yes!" the wife called out. "Jan is a mean guy. He's no good, I'm telling you. He's always lying to me, too."

"Ah," said Jan, "you impertinent woman!"

He took a knife and stabbed her. The blood spurted out and she fell backwards.

"Well, Jan," said the landlord, "look at that spectacle; you've stabbed your wife to death."

"Oh sir," said Jan, "take no notice of it. It's nothing, really."

He took an ordinary pennywhistle, blew it three times, and then his wife came back to life.

"Gosh, Jan, you should sell that whistle to me."

"No," said Jan, "no way."

"Oh, please."

"Well," said Jan, "for a thousand guilders you can have the whistle."

Then the landlord did something he normally never did: He went to the inn, drank until he was drunk, and then went home.

His wife said, "Man, have you lost your senses? What's the meaning of such vulgar behaviour? First you slaughter two perfectly good fat milk cows at the same time, and then you squander all the money at the inn. It's a disgrace!"

"Shut up, woman, or I'll stab you to death."

He very much felt like doing so, now that he had the whistle to blow on to bring her back to life.

He argued so long that his wife said, "You're drunk, man!"

And then he stabbed her to death.

It's nothing, he thought, and blew the whistle. Three times, six times, and more, but it was of no avail: The woman was really dead. In anger he rushed to Jan's.

"Jan, you cheat, you lied about everything again."

Jan had seen him coming again. There was a pot of pea soup bubbling on the fire.

"Wife," he said, "the landlord is coming. Put the pot behind the door quickly. The soup will continue cooking, it is very close to the boil."

"Jan, what have you got there in that pot that's boiling so much?"

"Sir, we always cook in that magic pot without any fire. We put the pot behind the door and it will cook by itself."

"How much do you ask for that pot? 'Cause now my wife is dead, the maid will have to do all the work on her own and she will find it very easy to cook with the pot without any fire."

"Yes," Jan said, "a bag full of money, 'cause such a pot is worth a lot. From now on, I'll have to buy wood and peat again continuously."

The landlord took the pot home with him and told the maid to just put the potatoes and the other food into it and then put the pot behind the door, so it would be well done by itself.

Yes, the maid thought, I bet Jan has played you another one of his tricks. But she was obedient and put the pot behind the door. She took a look inside it from time to time, but the potatoes stayed as raw as ever they were. When the landlord came home in the afternoon and wanted to have his dinner, he saw that Jan had deceived him and that the pot was as common as could be.

He went back to Jan again. "This is the absolute limit! You deceived me again! Now I've lost my patience. I think you'll have to be drowned."

He and his servant tied Jan up inside a bag and dragged him towards the water, but because this was quite a heavy load, the landlord first took his servant to the inn to have a glass of beer with him. For the time being, they left Jan in the bag near the water. Jan had heard everything, but could not get out of the bag.

He started calling out inside the bag, "Who wants to marry the king's daughter?"

And then again.

Then a farmer with a flock of sheep came by. He walked up to the bag and said to Jan, "I would want to."

"All right," Jan said. "I didn't want to and for that reason they want to drown me now. Please open the bag."

So the farmer did and crawled inside the bag, which Jan closed firmly.

The men returned from the inn and the farmer cried as loud as he could, "Yes, I want to!"

And then they said, "It's just as well that you want to, 'cause you're gonna have to anyway."

And so they tossed him into the water and the farmer drowned. In the meantime, Jan had gone home with the sheep. In the afternoon, Jan encountered the landlord.

"Heavens above, Jan, where do you come from? Is it really you?"

"Oh yes," said Jan, "I'll tell you where I come from. Down there in that canal there were so many, absolutely wonderful things! It's hardly to be believed, they wanted to give me so many things. Even a carriage with six horses, but I couldn't get that out on my own."

"Oh, you idiot," the landlord said. "I could help you with that, right?"

"Okay," said Jan, "just you crawl inside this bag; I will soon hop in too."

The landlord crawled into the bag. Jan rolled it into the water and the landlord drowned.

This story contains versions of ATU 1535, *The Rich and the Poor Farmer*, and ATU 1539, *Cleverness and Gullibility*. The tale was sent to collector G. J. Boekenoogen on January 22, 1894, by Mrs. S. H. Junius from Arnhem (Gelderland). The translation is based on T. Meder and C. Hendriks, *Vertelcultuur in Nederland* (Amsterdam, 2005), pp. 182–185.

THE MAN WHO FELL FROM HEAVEN

A simple, kind-hearted farmer's wife saw a young man standing somewhere along the country road. The man was staring at the sky while he cried and moaned.

The compassionate heart of the woman was touched, and she asked, "What's wrong with you, dear?"

"Oh, old mother, I fell from heaven and now I can't find back the hole!"

"You fell from heaven?" she repeated while shaking her head. "In that case, you'll know some people above."

"Of course."

"Oh, then perhaps you know my son too, good old Kees*?"

"What do you know; is he your son? He's my next door neighbour! Sure I know Kees!"

"So, how is he doing, that good and innocent boy?"

"Not bad, not bad. Only, the other week he was complaining that all of his stockings were worn-out, and he was out of sausages, ham, and butter. For the rest, he is doing just fine."

The old mother requested the young man to carry some goods to her son Kees, since he intended to return to heaven anyhow. The young man agreed. The woman prepared two parcels; one for the fallen young man and one—the best—for her son.

The young man left, but it is said that he still hasn't found the hole from which he fell to earth.

*Kees is a very common Dutch name.

This story is a version of ATU 1540, *The Student from Paradise (Paris)*—often the tale begins with some kind of misunderstanding, such as a student saying he comes from Paris, while the farmer thinks he said paradise. The tale was sent to collector G. J. Boekenoogen on February 7, 1894, by A. Rührup, a manufacturer of mineral water and lemonade from Rotterdam (South Holland). The translation is based on T. Meder and C. Hendriks, *Vertelcultuur in Nederland* (Amsterdam, 2005), p. 280.

THE LONG SPRING

A farmer had a great many sausages, hams, and sides of bacon hanging in the smoker. And yet his wife had to buy meat constantly.

"But husband, why won't you let me use that sausage?"

"Well, wife, because it's for the long spring."

The wife said, "For the Long Spring? Who on earth may that be?"

After a while, she asked again, but the answer was and remained, "For the long spring."

The wife did not understand, but a certain person who heard about it one day had a better understanding. He was tall and willing to try to impersonate this Long Spring.

He entered the house when the farmer was not home and said, "Well, woman, here I am to collect the sausage and the bacon."

"But who are you?"

"Me? I'm the Long Spring!"

"Well, well, are you the Long Spring! Well, if you must, there you have it!"

And the man took to his heels with those lovely sausages.

The farmer came home, missed the sausages of course, and heard from his wife what had happened. The farmer immediately saddled his best horse and rode after this Long Spring, in the direction his wife had shown him. When he arrived at the forest, the Long Spring had already seen him coming.

Long Spring threw aside his pack of meat and walked towards the farmer.

He asked, "What's the hurry, man?"

"Haven't you seen anybody around here with a heavy pack?"

"Yes, I have. He has just walked into the forest."

"But how can I enter the forest with my horse?"

"Well, I can mind your horse just for now."

In a jiffy, the farmer had disappeared into the forest, and in just as little time, the Long Spring sat on the horse with his sausages, and off he went.

This tale is a version of ATU 1541, *For the Long Winter.* The story was sent to collector G. J. Boekenoogen on February 7, 1894, by A. Rührup, a manufacturer of mineral water and lemonade from Rotterdam (South Holland). The translation is based on T. Meder and C. Hendriks, *Vertelcultuur in Nederland* (Amsterdam, 2005), pp. 280–281.

THE FARMER AND THE LAWYER

*T*here once was a farmer who had stolen four sheep. The police found out, the sheep were confiscated, and the farmer had to stand trial.

The farmer went to a lawyer and said, "I was caught stealing four sheep. I will have to stand trial. Will you defend me?"

"All right," the lawyer said, "I will defend you. But it will cost you 300 guilders."

"That's fine by me," the farmer replied.

"Well," the lawyer continued, "when you have to appear in court, you must pretend to be crazy. When the judge asks you a question, you must say, 'Baa!' "

"Okay," the farmer said.

He went to court and the judge asked him a question.

"Baa!" the farmer replied.

The judge asked him another question.

"Baa!" the farmer said.

And the third time, again, he said, "Baa!"

Then they were all convinced he was an idiot, and he was released.

As the farmer walked out of the courthouse, the lawyer was already waiting for him.

"I would like to have my 300 guilders now," the lawyer said.

"Baa!" the farmer said.

"You fool," the lawyer said, "you don't have to do that anymore."

"Baa!" said the farmer. He said "baa!" to everything, and the lawyer did not know what to do.

He never got his 300 guilders.

This version of ATU 1585, *The Lawyer's Mad Client*, was told in Drachten (Friesland) by the working-class storyteller Hendrik Meijer on April 3, 1969, and was recorded by collector A. A. Jaarsma (unpublished; Jaarsma Collection, report 619, tale no. 1; archive and Dutch Folktale Database, Meertens Instituut, Amsterdam).

I AM SO . . .

One day Tijl Uilenspiegel* was lying on the side of the road and he kept on crying, "Oh, I am so . . . . Oh, I am so . . . ."

This lamenting went on and on.

Several people came to have a look, because they thought he was seriously ill. In the end, they picked him up, brought him home, and put him to bed.

As soon as he lay down, he started yawning and finished his sentence, "Oh, I am so . . . . Oh, I am so . . . lazy!"

---

*Since the late Middle Ages Tijl Uilenspiegel has been a well-known trickster in Dutch literature and oral tradition.

This story belongs to an elaborate cycle of trickster tales about Tijl Uilenspiegel, internationally known as ATU 1635*, *Eulenspiegel's tricks*. In the catalogue of Frisian folktales by Jurjen van der Kooi this is number 31, "*O, wat ben ik . . . .*" ("Oh, I am so . . . .") . The Frisian version of the tale was told on September 14, 1970, to collector A. A. Jaarsma by Mrs. Bontje Kuipers-Veenstra, living in Drachten (Friesland). The translation is based on the (unpublished) manuscript of the Jaarsma Collection, report 826, tale no. 4 (archive and Dutch Folktale Database, Meertens Instituut, Amsterdam).

HANNES AND THE STATUE OF SAINT ANTHONY

*O*nce upon a time, there was a very stupid farmer, whose name was Hannes. He had a wife who was much cleverer than he was. For this reason, she was usually the one who ruled the entire household. She did the buying and selling and managed all the activities going on at the farm. But one day she had an accident that prevented her from walking, and thus was forced to stay at home.

The farmer had a cow that had to be sold, so now the man had no other option than to go to the market himself. The market would be held in a certain village at a few hours' distance from the house. It was decided that Hannes would go to the market with the cow. Several days before, the farmer's wife told her husband insistently how to act in case some merchants came to him to bargain over the cow and how the price should then be set.

"You must not," she said, "talk too much, 'cause then people might notice how stupid you are. Also avoid talkers, for talkers are no buyers. Now be sensible for once and insist on the price I have set. If people are not willing to pay enough for it, bring the cow back home. However, I'd rather you sold it, for you know we need the money to pay the rent. Oh, I wish I could go myself. How terrible it is to have such a stupid husband," the farmer's wife added, sighing.

These words upset Hannes a bit. So he decided to act in such a way that his wife would be pleased with him. The next morning the farmer left for the market with the cow. Market day was well-attended and there were many people interested in the cow. The animal was handled a lot. But the merchants were very talkative, and Hannes didn't like that. They offered money and made a lot of fuss, but the farmer wasn't interested in these talkative guys, bearing in mind the words of his wife: talkers are no buyers.

Hannes remained silent as the grave.

Whenever he was asked what he thought of their offers, he turned his head and said, "You can't have the cow."

So the merchants cleared off in the end, leaving the farmer on his own in the market.

Well, he thought, I suppose I'd better leave too now. There won't be any merchants about who are not talkative anyway. But what will the wife say when I bring the cow back home? She'll call me stupid all the more, even though I've done exactly what she said.

Thus the farmer walked back home with the cow. On his way home, he passed through a small village and alongside a small church, which happened to have its doors open at the time. He quite fancied having a look inside to see if there was a merchant who was not so talkative. As it happened, there had been a pilgrimage that day. People had been worshipping the statue of Saint Anthony with the pig to prevent contagious pig disease. It was late and the church was empty. The farmer entered the church with the cow. He tied the cow to a church bench and walked on, for he had discovered someone who stood very still and didn't speak a word, namely the statue of Saint Anthony with the pig. The statue had been placed high up against the wall and was dressed in actual monk's clothes. (In the early days, statues of saints were dressed in clothes of actual fabric.)

Since the farmer lived at quite a distance from any town or village, he seldom went to church. Perhaps he had been there only a couple of times in his entire life. So he didn't know anything about these statues. He thought, this must be a pig merchant. Surely he'll be interested in buying the cow as well. Besides, he's standing still and doesn't say a word. This is the right man.

He stood right in front of the statue, nodded, and called out, "Come down, my friend! Then I will sell you my cow. She is right over there; a fine animal, I'm telling you."

There was total silence.

"How much for the cow? Please, tell me straight how much she's worth to you. No need to make a fuss about it. Just say it in one single word, please!"

Again, there was total silence.

"Well, just you be silent then. After all, my wife doesn't like talkers. Just nod yes or no when I tell you the price of the cow. Would you want her for 160 guilders?"

Total silence followed. Now our little peasant got angry. He took his stick and knocked the statue off its base, so it ended up rolling on the floor in front of him. And with the statue, a bag of money came falling down.

"There you are," said the farmer, "I knew you'd be sensible. If only you had spoken, I wouldn't have hit you."

The farmer picked up the money and left the church. He left the cow behind. He arrived home with 500 guilders. With a wide grin on his face, he threw the money into his wife's lap.

"There you are," he said, "I don't think you'll still say Hannes is so stupid, now will you?"

His wife counted the money and was surprised at the large amount. She asked how he had managed to get so much money for the cow, and how the merchant looked, for she just could not believe people had become so generous and that Hannes had become so clever all of a sudden.

Hannes didn't speak much about what had happened in the church, for he thought, if I tell her I beat the merchant, she'll scold me. So he only told her he was a pig merchant and that he had thrown the bag of money at his feet. That was it.

But what happened in the church in the meantime? The sexton came to lock up the church and found the cow tied to the bench. When he had another look around, he noticed that the statue of Saint Anthony had fallen off its base. The sexton's heart missed a beat; he had hidden his savings in the back of the statue. He thought they'd be safe in there. The fact of the matter is that the sexton had a wife who spent all the money, whereas he, by contrast, was very economical. He occasionally got a tip from someone, and he had his old age to consider. After all, one day he would no longer be able to practise his profession. It had taken him a long time to gather so much money, and now it was all gone. What was he to do? And this cow in the church; what on earth was the meaning of that? He was beginning to think this must be some miracle, for how else was something as peculiar as this to be explained? After having paced about in thought and searching for some time, he decided to call in the priest. The sexton told him about the money and all the other things. The priest couldn't make sense of it either. Normally speaking, one would suspect this to be the work of thieves, but in that case, where did the cow come from? Thieves are not in the habit of giving anything in return. What could have happened?

Then he remembered that there had been a market at an hour's distance from the village.

Surely some thief had stolen the cow there, and, when he no longer felt safe, left the cow behind in the church. He must have run off, taking the money with him. One way or the other, he must have discovered the money. They did not as yet have a clue how, but it could have been someone known to them, who could have spied on the sexton when he was busy with the money. These were, in a nutshell, the ideas of the priest and the sexton on the matter.

"Yes," said the priest, "let's quickly go to the country policeman, so that he can pursue the thief."

"No," said the sexton, "don't do that. Don't create any publicity in the matter. It's got to be hushed up, for if my wife knew, she would laugh at me into the bargain. And on top of that, I could never save anything anymore."

"Well," said the priest, "in that case, take the cow home with you and say to your wife that it is a gift from me. That will give you some compensation for the money you've lost."

It was no sooner said than done. The sexton arrived home with the cow. His wife was somewhat surprised at such a gift, all the more so because the priest was usually quite economical, and pretty short of money anyway. The sexton, however, persuaded her by saying that if she didn't believe him, she ought to ask the priest about it herself.

The cow was put in the shed. And would you believe it, the wife was actually pleased with the animal and took very good care of it. This gave her something to do, and instead of having coffee parties and paying visits to her neighbours all the time, she was now constantly busy with the cow. The cow was very profitable, for it was a fine animal. The woman became thrifty now that she realized she could actually make some money. In this way, they made some savings, and bought another cow and a piece of land. At present, the sexton is a wealthy man possessing a large flock of cattle and lots of land. Since all this has happened, Hannes too is much better thought of by his wife than ever before. No more remarks about his stupidity. Ever. Now the wife can pay off her debts and even have some money left over.

In this way, two households have become very happy due to the sexton's savings.

This tale is a version of ATU 1643, *Money inside the Statue*. The story was sent to collector G. J. Boekenoogen in 1894 by Mrs. Cornelis from Rotterdam (South Holland). The translation is based on T. Meder, *De magische vlucht* (Amsterdam, 2000), pp. 239–243.

THE POLE OF
OOSTERLITTENS

*O*nce upon a time, there lived a shoemaker in Oosterlittens who was always short of money. He worked hard, his wife was sparing, but a growing number of children forced him to cut his coat according to his cloth.

Nevertheless, the shoemaker was convinced that there were better times to come.

One morning he said to his wife, "Last night I had a dream that I would find my fortune at the Papenbrug* in Amsterdam."

"It's a good thing that Amsterdam is not next door," the woman replied. "You would be foolish enough to go there. Dreams are a delusion, remember?"

The shoemaker kept silent about it, but the whole day long he was unable to get this dream out of his head.

The next night he had the same dream again, that he would find his fortune in Amsterdam on the Papenbrug. He thought this might be a sign, and he mentioned it to his wife once more. However, she laughed right in his face and refused to talk about it.

The third night, the shoemaker had the same dream once more. That morning, his mind was made up. No matter what his wife said, it could not prevent him from packing his suitcase and setting out on his journey.

In Amsterdam, he asked directions for the Papenbrug. Once there, he walked around a bit, without knowing exactly what to look for. The first day he found nothing. The second day he found nothing again.

On the evening of the third day, just as he was about to return to his guesthouse empty-handed, a beggar walked up to him.

"I could not help noticing," he said, "that you've been wandering about for three days now. Are you looking for something?"

"I'll tell you," the shoemaker said. "At home I had the same dream three nights in a row. I dreamt that here on the Papenbrug I would find my fortune."

The beggar started laughing and said, "So you are such a fool that you believe in dreams? I don't. A short while ago I had such a peculiar dream three nights in a row, too. I dreamt that in the middle of a meadow behind the house of a shoemaker, who lives opposite

---

the church of Oosterlittens in Friesland, there is a pole and at the very same spot a pot of money is buried. Am I crazy enough to travel to this place? No way!"

The shoemaker didn't bat an eyelid.

"It's probably for the best that I go home," he said.

Once home, he started digging immediately. His wife called him names, but as soon as he pulled a pot full of money out of the hole, her temper vanished.

"Well?" the shoemaker said. "Didn't I tell you that I had to go to the Papenbrug in Amsterdam to find my fortune?"

She had to admit he was right. They agreed to keep the discovery a secret. The treasure was saved for a rainy day and the pot was used with the other household goods.

There was an inscription on the pot, but they couldn't read it, because it was in a foreign language.

One day the minister came to visit them. As he sat down near the fireplace, he spotted the pot hanging above the fire. He looked at the inscription and asked where the pot had come from.

"I bought it from an iron merchant," the shoemaker said.

"Do you know what is written here?" the minister asked.

"No," said the shoemaker. "I don't understand the language."

"It's Latin," the minister said. "It reads, 'underneath this pot there is another one.' I just don't understand what it means."

"Neither do I," the shoemaker said.

However, as soon as the minister had left, the shoemaker started digging so hard that the lumps of earth flew through the air. Indeed, he found another pot, filled to the rim with money. Now he was a very wealthy man.

As a memorial to his fortune, the shoemaker replaced the wooden pole in his back yard with a stone one. More than a hundred years after his death the stone pole was still standing there.

---

*The name of a bridge over a canal in Amsterdam.

This tale is a version of ATU 1645, *The Treasure at Home*. The story was collected by the Frisian collector Waling Dykstra at the end of the nineteenth century. The translation is based on E. de Jong and P. Klaasse, *Sagen en Legenden van de Lage Landen* (Bussum, 1980), pp. 13–17.

MAYOR OX

*O*nce upon a time, there was a rich farmer, who was as thick as a brick. He had no children, but he did own an ox and a donkey. The farmer had often heard that one could become really smart at the university, and this idea intrigued him more every day.

One day, a prankster said to him, "Well, would you believe that they can even turn stupid animals into intelligent human beings at the university?"

"You don't say . . . ," the farmer replied. "Well, in that case I would like to try it. My ox is so bright that if I say 'giddyup, giddyup' to the donkey, the ox is already walking in the right direction."

So the farmer took his ox to the university. I suppose he went to Leyden. Once there, the farmer rang a doorbell at random and a student opened the door. The farmer said that he wanted to see the professor, because he wanted to sign up his ox for university. Well, the student didn't go for any professor, but informed a senior student.

The senior went to the farmer and said to him, "It's okay, my friend, you can leave your ox here."

The farmer asked how much that would cost him.

"Seventy guilders."

The farmer paid and the ox stayed in Leyden. After a month, the farmer thought, I should pay the ox a visit to see how he is coming along. He travelled to Leyden, but the ox wasn't home; he had gone to class. The farmer learned that the ox was making much progress, but more money was needed. That's how it went, every time the farmer came to Leyden.

After the farmer had paid like this for a year and a half, without even seeing his beloved animal once, he became mad and demanded his ox back.

"That's funny," the student said. "Didn't he write to you then? He has to do his exams, and I suppose he will pass, but it will cost you money."

"Oh, all right then," the farmer conceded, "but this will be the last time."

So he paid another hundred guilders. Since he still got neither word nor sign from the ox, he returned to Leyden once more, determined to take him back home. He met the same student again.

"I don't understand," the student said. "Did he fail to write to you once more? He passed his exam and he has already found a splendid job: He became mayor of Amsterdam."

"The rascal!" the farmer exclaimed. "I'll get him for that, wait and see!"

So he went to Amsterdam. It so happened that the mayor was called Ox. The farmer rang his doorbell and asked if the mayor was home.

"Yes," the servant answered, and asked what the farmer wanted.

"Well," the farmer said. "I am his boss and I want to take him home."

Of course, the servant did not understand a word and thought the farmer was a lunatic. The two started arguing. Then the mayor himself arrived and told the servant to keep calm. The farmer was allowed inside.

Well, then he had to tell about his ox and the university, and finally he said, "I will put on your bridle now, to take you home, so that the wife can see you."

Even for the mayor this went way too far, and he threw the farmer out.

Dispirited, the farmer went back home, and when he arrived, he said to his wife, "Truly, there are clever people in Leyden, because our ox turned into a learned man. Still, there's no benefit or joy in it,

For if a nobody
Becomes somebody
It spells sorrow for everybody."

This tale is a version of ATU 1675, *The Ox (Ass) as Mayor*. The story was told to collector C. Bakker by dairy farmer Dirk Schuurman in Broek in Waterland (North Holland) on October 2, 1901. The translation is based on T. Meder, *Vertelcultuur in Waterland* (Amsterdam, 2001), pp. 295–296.

JAN AND TRIJNTJE

*J*an and Trijntje lived under a chamber pot. One night there was such a violent storm that the pot was blown over and broke. Jan, who wasn't very eloquent, was stammering a bit.

He said, "Us leave and ask shelter at the nearest farmer."

"Okay," Trijntje said.

They knocked on the door of a farmer's house. "Would there be any room for us?"

"Sure."

But because Jan was such a gigantic eater, Trijntje said to him, "When I kick your foot, make sure you put your spoon down."

"All right, Trijntje," Jan said.

But this farmer also had a tremendously fat dog.

When they were having their meals, this dog walked past them under the table and kicked Jan's foot. Jan threw down his spoon in anger. He thought, Well, Trijntje, now you won't have any more either. And he kicked Trijntje's foot.

In the early days, there were beds and box beds next to each other in the room. When they all went to bed, the farmer and his wife were in one bed, and Jan and Trijntje in the other.

Then Jan said, "Why you kick my foot?"

"I didn't do that," Trijntje said, "it must have been the dog. But why did you kick my foot?"

"I thought," he said, "you wouldn't have any more either."

Then Trijntje said, "I know where the porridge is kept. I'll first eat my stomach full in the cellar, and then I'll return to you with a big spoonful."

In the early days there were tremendously large kettles of porridge. Trijntje ate her stomach full in the cellar and then returned with a large spoon full of porridge. But she walked over to the wrong bed! The one the farmer and his wife were in. And the farmer was just about to break wind.

"Pprrff!" said the farmer.

Jan and Trijntje   213

"My dear Jan," Trijntje said, "it isn't hot."

A brief silence followed.

"Pprrff!" said the farmer.

"But Jan," she said, 'there's no need to blow."

But the farmer said, "Pprrf!"

Then she said, "If you do that again, Jan, I'll smack you on the butt with this spoon full of porridge."

A moment later, there was the sound again. "Pprrff!" said the farmer.

And then she decided to hit him. She smacked him on the butt with the spoon full of porridge, and the porridge went flying in all directions. It was only then that she noticed she was standing next to the wrong bed.

"Jan, Jan, quickly, run," she called.

In the old days, there were doors consisting of two halves, and Jan rammed out the entire lower half of the door in his flight.

Trijntje said, "Take it along, take it along, Jan, it'll give us a roof over our heads."

All right, along came the door.

In the forest, there was a large oak tree, which they climbed into. They held the door over their heads. There came along three robbers. They had a huge heap of money with them. Under the tree, they began to divide the loot.

After a while, Trijntje said, "I have to take a leak."

"Well," said Jan, "just pee downwards."

The robbers said, "Heavenly water is falling down."

Some time later, she had to do a number two.

Then she said, "Jan, I have to relieve myself."

"Just shit downwards," Jan said.

Thereupon the robbers said, "Heavenly mustard is falling down."

Some time later, Jan said, "I can no longer hold on to this door, Trijntje!"

Trijntje then said, "Just drop it."

He threw the door down.

Then the robbers said, "Heavenly doors are falling down!"

And then they became so frightened that they ran for it and left all the money. The couple climbed out of the tree and took the money along.

"There we are," Jan said, "this will hire us a nice farm, Trijntje!"

They hired a nice farm, but Jan didn't know how to milk the cows. Trijntje had to do the milking. One morning they came home to see the cows lying in the field, ruminating satisfactorily.

Then she said, "Jan, when I come to the animals in the morning, they are constantly taking the piss out of me." And she added, "If they do it again, I'll cut all their heads off tomorrow morning."

Thereupon she sharpened the knife. The next morning, the animals were lying in the field again, ruminating contently. Believe it or not, she then cut off all the animals' heads!

They had now come to the point that they had only one side of bacon left.

Jan said, "We should keep that for the long splinter."

He meant, for the long winter. While Jan was out, a tall, skinny fellow came along.

Trijntje asked, "Are you the long Splinter?"

"Yes," the guy replied.

"Well, Jan did say there is one side of bacon left, and you should have it."

Jan returned home that night.

She said, "I gave the last side of bacon to the long Splinter."

"Dear," Jan said, "now we have nothing left."

So then Jan and Trijntje were forced to go back and live under the chamber pot again.

This story contains versions of ATU 1691, *The Hungry Clergyman*; ATU 1653, *The Robbers under the Tree*; ATU 1211, *The Cow Chewing Its Cud*; and ATU 1541, *For the Long Winter*. The tale was told in September 1971 to collector Ype Poortinga by the Frisian storyteller and mole catcher Anders Bijma from Boelenslaan. He got the story from his grandfather, Alle Bijma. The translation from Frisian is based on T. Meder, *De magische vlucht* (Amsterdam, 2000), pp. 227–230.

YOU SHOULDN'T HAVE DONE THAT

*P*ieterke had to get a darning needle for his mother. He stuck the needle in a hay cart. When he came home, the darning needle was missing.

His mother said, "My dear Pieterke, how could you do such a thing? You should have pinned it on your jacket!"

"Next time I will do it like that," said Pieterke.

Then he had to fetch a pitchfork, which he stuck on his jacket.

When he came home, his mother said, "You shouldn't have done that; you should have dragged it along behind you!"

"Next time I will do it like that," said Pieterke.

Then he had to get a piece of ham, which he dragged along behind him. And the dogs ate it.

When he came home his mother said, "You shouldn't have done it like that; you should have carried it on your head!"

"Next time I will do it like that!" said Pieterke.

Then he had to collect some syrup, which he carried on his head. When he came home, his entire face was covered in syrup.

His mother said, "That does it!"

Then his mother came after him, and Pieterke crawled inside a barrel full of feathers. But all the feathers were sticking to his head.

When he came out he was a rooster, calling, "Cock-a-doodle-doo, cock-a-doo-dle-doo."

The tale is a version of ATU 1696, *"What should I have said (done)?"* This story was sent to collector G. J. Boekenoogen in May 1892 by J. van der Veen from Amsterdam (North Holland), but the tale is said to originate from Terschelling (Friesland). The translation is based on T. Meder, *De magische vlucht* (Amsterdam, 2000), p. 230.

DIVIDING NUTS IN THE CHURCHYARD

*O*nce upon a time there were two brothers. One was wise, and the other was mad. Together they had stolen a bag full of nuts.

The wise one said to the mad brother, "While you divide the nuts, I will steal that sheep we saw walking in the meadow."

"All right," said the mad one, "I'll make sure I'll find a nice and safe place for us to divide the loot."

He went into the churchyard and climbed over the wall of the bone shed (where they keep dead men's bones). In this shed, he started to divide the nuts. Every time he took two nuts out of the bag, he put them on two different piles.

With each two he said, "That one is for me, that one is for you."

The sexton, who was still in the church despite the late hour, heard a noise from inside the churchyard. He listened and heard that the sound came from the bone shed. He listened again and clearly heard the following words, "That one is for me, that one is for you."

With a distraught look on his face and pale with fear, the sexton went to the priest's and said, "Oh Father, never, nevermore dare I tread into the church! Would this be the end of days? I believe the angels and the devils are counting the bones. Clearly I heard it said, repeatedly, 'That one is for me, that one is for you'."

"Oh come on, you daft idiot!" said the Father, "is your head haunted too? I don't believe a word of all your tales."

The sexton said, "Father, if you won't come along with me to see what is going on, I dare never go inside the church anymore."

The Father, an old man suffering from rheumatism, joined the sexton and went to the church, leaning on his walking stick. And wouldn't you know, from inside the churchyard, he also heard, repeatedly, "That one is for me, that one is for you."

"But," said the Father, "I may have heard it now, but I'd also like to see it."

"Not me, Father! Upon my soul! Not me."

"Well, I'm not asking you to have a look," said the Father, "but that wall is too high for me. If you'd be kind enough to lean over for me, I can climb on your back. Then I will be able to look inside the bone shed."

The sexton was willing to agree to that, and when the Father was standing on his back, he could just about peek over the edge of the wall.

But the noise they were making had alarmed the mad one, who thought he heard his brother, and said, "Ah, there you are! Wait, let's be quick about this and cut that throat immediately!"

The sexton got the shock of his life: He thought they were talking about HIS throat. He took to his heels and dropped the Father. And this good man, who had been muddling along with his rheumatism for many, many years, was so scared that he could walk straight again, just like that.

This story is known as folktale type ATU, *The Sexton Carries the Parson*, and was sent to collector G. J. Boekenoogen in 1894 by Mrs. Deenik from Haarlem (North Holland). The translation is based on T. Meder, *De magische vlucht* (Amsterdam, 2000), pp. 235–236.

THE SAWN-THROUGH PULPIT

*O*ne day a carpenter wanted to play a trick on the local clergyman when he was standing at the pulpit. On a weekday, he sawed through most of the lower part of the pulpit, just for the fun of it. He thought that when the clergyman ascended the pulpit, it would collapse in its entirety. But imagine his disappointment when it didn't come down.

The carpenter thought, of course, I didn't saw it through well enough. I'll give it another go this week.

After having sawn it through a bit more, the carpenter was back in the church the next Sunday. Immediately after the clergyman had ascended the pulpit, he came falling down, taking the entire construction with him.

The carpenter exclaimed, "I had expected you last week!"

This joke is known as folktale type ATU 1825C, *The Sawed Pulpit*, and was sent to collector G. J. Boekenoogen in March 1894 by G. Poot from Loosduinen (South Holland). The translation is based on T. Meder, *De magische vlucht* (Amsterdam, 2000), p. 236.

SPOON AS PROOF

 parish priest had a visit from a friend. After dinner, he showed his friend the entire house.

After he had gone, the maid said, "I thought you invited a decent guest for dinner."

"Why do you say that?"

"Well, he stole a silver spoon."

Some time later, the same friend visited the priest again, and the priest said, "The maid told me that you stole a spoon."

"I say," said the friend, "didn't you find it then?"

"No," the maid said, "and I have looked everywhere."

"Really?" the visitor exclaimed. "Do you want to know where it is?"

They all climbed up to the maid's room.

The friend turned over the sheets in the maid's bed, and there lay the spoon, untouched.

Now the friend said to the priest, "I just wanted to know whether the maid sleeps with you, or you sleep with the maid."

This joke is a version of ATU 1842C*, *The Rector's Nights*. Collector G. J. Boekenoogen recorded this joke in Leyden (South Holland) at the end of the nineteenth century. The translation is based on T. Meder and C. Hendriks, *Vertelcultuur in Nederland* (Amsterdam, 2005), p. 460.

A LIE

A blind man saw a millstone floating
up the stream—it's not a jest.
A lame man jumped into the water,
and laid it on a bank to rest.
A naked man put the millstone in
the pocket of his Sunday best.

This short rhyme of lies is a version of ATU 1965, *The Disabled Comrades*. It was sent to collector G. J. Boekenoogen at the end of the nineteenth century by Mrs. G. Niemeyer, who lived in Hilversum (North Holland). Without the title it can be used as a riddle as well, by asking "What is that?" Answer, "A lie." The translation is based on T. Meder and C. Hendriks, *Vertelcultuur in Nederland* (Amsterdam, 2005), pp. 226–227.

BAUKE THE SKATER

*T*he storyteller's grandfather used to tell him about a man who could skate incredibly fast. His name was Bauke.* He worked somewhere in a small village, but he lived in the countryside, in the neighbourhood of Earnewâld. Once upon a time, he came home from his work in the afternoon and his mother had just prepared a meal of baked potatoes.

"I would like to have some mustard with that," Bauke said.

"We're all out of mustard," was the answer.

"No problem," Bauke said. "I'll just skate to Warten to buy me a pot of mustard. I will be on my way and back in no time; the potatoes won't even get cold."

So he put on his skates and raced over the Langeslaetten towards Warten. Somewhere on the side of the ditch, a boat was frozen into the ice. Bauke was skating extremely fast, taking very long strokes, and as he came alongside, he tipped the boat with one of his skates, so that the flatboat** started to spin in the ice like crazy.

He kept on skating, and in front of him was a hole in the ice. He did not notice the hole and fell in, full speed. He hit the other side of the hole with his neck, and it so happened that his head was cut off by the sharpness of the ice. While his head continued to slide on the ice, his body went on beneath the ice. A bit farther there was another hole, and there the head and the body reunited. Because of the severe frost, the head and the body froze together again.

Bauke managed to climb out of the hole and arrived in Warten, where he visited the small store to buy his mustard. As he walked out again, he noticed how cold it was and he realized that he had to skate for a considerable distance. So he decided to take a rest and have a drink in order to warm himself up a bit.

Bauke entered the local inn, where people were sitting around the fireplace. He joined them and after a while, his nose started running. He went for his handkerchief, but the hanky was so wet that it was of no use to him. So he had to blow his nose the old-fashioned way, just using his index finger and thumb. Due to the warmth, his head came loose again, without Bauke noticing. As he tried to blow his nose into the fire, he accidentally threw his whole head in the fireplace—believe it or not.

Then he skated home without his head. And the boat, which had started spinning after he had touched it with his skate earlier, had built up such speed that it was still going round and round when he passed it on his way back home.

---

*This is a typical Frisian man's name.

**The Frisian "skûtsje" has a flat bottom with hardly any keel.

This humorous tall tale is known as VDK 1970*, *Afgesneden hoofd vriest weer vast aan de romp* (Cut-off head freezes to body again). It was told to collector Ype Poortinga on January 12, 1972, by Dirk Wiersma in Grouw (Friesland). Wiersma was director of the Frisian educational radio. The translation from Frisian is based on Ype Poortinga, *De foet fan de reinbôge* (Baarn, 1979), p. 383.

THE MOSQUITOES OF DALFSEN

*O*n a bright summer evening the people from Dalfsen were sitting outside their doors having a chat. Some of them strolled along the Koffiestraatje* in the sultry air. Here and there, children played with their tops and hoops. People drank a cool pint of lager and ate a local cookie. Then, all of a sudden, a man's voice said in a tranquil fashion, "Fire in the church tower. Fire!"

The inhabitants of Dalfsen were delicate people, not accustomed to nasty events.

They turned their heads towards the tower. Some had a house blocking their view, while others were too sleepy to look, but the rest looked.

"Fire!" the man yelled, and now he pointed his shaking finger in the direction of the tower that rose high and slender above all the other tall buildings. "Fire! In the tower! Can't you see those smoky clouds . . . ?! Help!"

A crowd gathered and people bumped into each other. Well, yes . . . people saw the narrow cloud of smoke whirling around the tower in a menacing fashion . . . . It blew about and grew again, it became dark, and then it faded for a while against the vivid blue of the summer evening sky.

Women started to scream, as they should during disasters. The children cheered because they understood they didn't have to go to bed.

The men, the serious dutiful men of Dalfsen, walked to the banks of the river Vecht with swift, distinguished steps.

Two men laid down on their bellies near the lower ends of the bridge and scooped up the water into their hands. Because it was such a hot summer, they had left their hats at home.

Others stood next to them, stalping with haste and sorrow, and many looked up in fearful misery to the narrow cloud so high above the village.

Quickly, extinguish the fire, before the tower crashes into the village! Too many farms were made of wood.

Some people started to panic and call for their children, who had obviously made themselves scarce. Others started to shout for help for themselves, before it would be too

---

late. Some people went to pack their jewels and money in suitcases, in order to escape the village, which they thought was in roaring flames already.

Many fell on their knees in the middle of the street and eagerly prayed to all the powers they could remember from catechism, relics and songs from the fair. At this precious moment, many people realized they had lived a sinful life in this tidy little town, accumulating debts, dancing in the bar, peeping at ladies with hungry looks: The horrific things one is forced to face when such a tower, clouded in doom, is pointing towards heaven like a finger.

Then, still within half an hour, the fire department arrived, in uniform, with polished shoes, wigs, and hats off, with only wet nightcaps on their heads, as prescribed. The firemen filled their buckets with water from the Vecht and passed them on to Gait, who gave them to Jan-Willem, while Jan-Willem gave them to Martijn, and then they went on to Willem, and to Peter, et cetera . . . until they were emptied in a large wooden tub. A beautiful, brand-new fire pump was installed in the tub. Four men pumped with swelling muscles, while another four aimed their gurgling fire hoses, like generals with terrifying arms.

It was such a moving sight. The suspense became unbearable. The mayor got stuck in the crowd, his instructions were no longer heard, and he lost his watch. He yelled something about remaining calm and about thieves, but he was misunderstood. Women tried to faint in the arms of handsome men, and children started throwing stones through windows, because everyone would blame it on the fire anyway. Two very old ladies began to cry with long howls in high-pitched voices. It was shocking to see how the community of Dalfsen shook like dice in a mug. Meanwhile, near the waterside, the firemen kept on working, sweaty and with crimson faces: Gait, Jan-Willem, Martijn, Peter, and all the others . . . .

The church tower stood very still, like an immense piece of fireworks, ready to explode.

"It's moving . . . !"

Men and women embraced each other in despair. The water from the fire hoses splattered much too low against the wall.

Now the mayor had lost one of his shoe buckles as well. Surrounded by a screaming crowd, he kept his hand on his wallet and shouted until his face turned purple.

"The tower!" roared a tall fellow who should be able to see best. "He's going down, folks! Clear off, clear off!"

Meanwhile, the firemen kept on handing over the buckets: Gait, Jan-Willem, Martijn, Peter . . . .

Then—much too calmly—a man showed up at the top of the tower. How could he have passed the fire?

He gesticulated like a minister, solemnly spreading his arms, not the least in a hurry to meet his Maker.

The man in the tower put his hands beside his mouth and called, "There is no fire . . . ! There are mosquitoes swarming around the tower!"

Now the jet of water from the fire hose lost its power altogether—the hose gargled.

Mosquitoes?! Swarming mosquitoes on a summer evening?

Thus the fear and curiosity faded away.

And among the inhabitants of Dalfsen there were some outsiders from Zwolle and Hoonhorst. While they tried to keep a straight face, they felt sarcastic mockery coming up.

"Mosquitoes!" "Mosquito sprayers!" the visitors said to each other.

Today you can ask any inhabitant of the province of Overijssel about the Mosquitoes, and his eyes will turn towards Dalfsen. For these kind of stories won't go away . . . .

---

*Coffee Street.

This tale is a version of TM 2602, *Spotnaam voor naburig dorp (stad) of hun inwoners* (nickname for neighbouring village [town] or their inhabitants). A similar story can be told about Meppel in the province of Drente and Haarlem in the province of North Holland. Another nickname for the people of Dalfsen is "moppen" (after their cookies). This translation of the folktale is based on R. A. Koman, *Dalfser Muggen* (Bedum, 2006), pp. 24–26.

MONKEY TRICK

*A*n entire family—father, mother, and children—went to the zoo. They wanted to see everything. Knowing that the children liked giving things to the animals, like sweets, peanuts, and so on, father and mother had brought a bag of fruit. Jantje, the eldest, was allowed to throw a peach into the monkey cage. To his utter amazement, the monkey first took the stone out and tried to stick it up his bum. Then he got it out again and ate it.

Jantje, surprised, asked, "Daddy, what's he doing?"

"Well," daddy said, "that monkey is sensible. He won't eat anything that won't come out at the back."

This story was sent to the Meertens Institute in 1991 by Kees Mommersteeg, a market gardener from Vlijmen (North Brabant). The translation is based on T. Meder, *De magische vlucht* (Amsterdam, 2000), p. 248.

A CLEVER DOG

A butcher was busy working when he noticed a dog in his shop; he chased it away. Several minutes later, he saw the dog was back again. He walked towards the dog and saw that it had a note in its mouth. It said, "2 pounds of minced meat, 2 steaks, 1 pound of pork, please."

The butcher looked again and noticed that the dog also had a 100-guilder note in its mouth. So the butcher prepared the order and put it into a plastic bag, together with the change. He hung the bag in the dog's mouth.

The butcher was very impressed, and since it was almost closing time anyway, he decided to close the shop and follow the dog. The dog walked on the pavement for a while until he reached a zebra crossing. He put the plastic bag down, jumped up against the traffic light post, pressed the button, took the bag into his mouth again, and waited patiently for the light to turn green. As soon as this happened, he crossed the street, with the butcher right behind him.

Then the dog arrived at a bus stop and began to study the timetable. The butcher's mouth opened wide with surprise. After having looked at the timetable, the dog sat down on the bench. The bus arrived; the dog walked to the front of the bus, looked at the route number, and returned to the bench. Another bus arrived, and again, the dog walked to the front of the bus. He saw this was the right bus and got on.

The butcher was flabbergasted. He followed the dog onto the bus. The bus drove around the town for a while and then entered the suburbs. At a certain moment, the dog got up, stood on his hind legs, and pressed the stop button, so that the bus would stop at the next stop. The dog got off, still carrying the shopping bag in his mouth. The butcher was still following him.

They walked along a small road and the dog approached a house. He walked up to the front door and put the shopping bag down. Then he walked a few yards back, took a running start, and threw himself against the front door. He waited a moment, walked a few yards back again, and threw himself against the front door again. Still nobody opened up. The dog walked to the beginning of the front garden, climbed on the surrounding wall, and walked across it to the side of the house. He approached a window and hit his head against it several times. He walked back across the wall, jumped down, walked to the front door, took the shopping bag into his mouth, and waited.

The butcher saw some guy opening the door. And would you believe it, he wouldn't stop cursing and swearing at the dog!

The butcher walked to the front door and said to this guy, "What are you playing at, you creep? This dog is a genius. You should go on TV with him instead of standing here swearing at him!"

Whereupon the guy answered, "This dog a genius, huh? I don't think so! This is the second time this week he forgot his keys!"

The joke was sent via e-mail by Luuk van Dongen, a student in Eindhoven (North Brabant), to his sister, Jeske van Dongen, who forwarded the joke to me on May 12, 1998. The translation is based on T. Meder, *De magische vlucht* (Amsterdam, 2000), pp. 248–250.

THE MAGICIAN AND THE PARROT

A magician had a job on a cruise ship. While he was performing his tricks, there was a parrot in the room observing him closely.

At a certain moment, the magician conjured up a deck of cards.

The parrot shouted, "He took that out of his right sleeve!"

A moment later the magician conjured up a bunch of flowers.

The parrot shouted, "He took that out of his inside pocket!"

All of a sudden, a vast blow was heard. The ship had hit a reef; it took on water and sank in no time at all.

The magician and the parrot were the only survivors of this disaster, and they sought refuge on the same piece of wreckage. There they sat, opposite to each other, looking at each other in silence.

After a while the parrot said, "I give up! Where did you leave the ship?"

_____

This joke was told in the first series of a Dutch television program called *Moppentoppers* (top jokers), RTL4, September–October 1994. It has been published in T. Meder, *De magische vlucht* (Amsterdam, 2000), p. 245.

THE SOCCER TALENT

*S*occer club Ajax was having serious problems. The team couldn't manage to score and was losing one game after the other.

One day, one of the scouts came up to the coach and told him that he had made a study trip to Iraq, where he discovered a fabulous soccer talent. Since the coach had hardly any other options left, he decided to have this sixteen-year-old talent come over to Amsterdam. During the first training the coach was so impressed by the young talent's play that he offered him a contract right away.

During the first match, the coach put the young player on the reserves' bench, but at half-time Ajax was already behind 4–0 and seemed unable to score, so in the last half hour of the game the coach brought in the Iraqi boy. Within thirty minutes he scored five goals, and Ajax won the game.

The boy left the field feeling mighty proud, and the first thing he wanted to do was call his mother. He took his cell phone, called his mother, and told her of his magnificent performance, but he noticed that his mother was unable to react enthusiastically.

Finally, he asked his mother, "Mother, I scored five times, aren't you happy for me?"

"Of course I am," his mother replied, "but there are terrible things happening over here. Your father got killed, and they have tried to rape your sister and me. It's a living hell out here."

"But mother," the boy answered, "you can't blame me for this?"

"Of course I can, my son. You made us move to Amsterdam!"

This joke was sent to me by e-mail on October 16, 2003, during the war in Iraq. The storyteller is Danny Plugge (born in Vlaardingen in 1961), who works as an office manager in Rotterdam. In a way, the joke deals with the rivalry between Amsterdam and Rotterdam, the two largest cities in the Netherlands. Rotterdam owns one of the largest sea harbours in the world and is proud to be a city of hardworking common people. The people of Amsterdam think of Rotterdam as a dull city without any culture or civilization. Amsterdam considers itself to be a centre of tolerance, history, and art, while the people of Rotterdam think of Amsterdam as a kind of Sodom and Gomorrah, where chaos and abuse rule. The capital of the Netherlands has the reputation of having a high crime rate, but for years now the statistics prove that the highest crime rates are to be found in Rotterdam. The joke is a direct translation of the e-mail; it has not been published before, but can be found in the Dutch Folktale Database of the Meertens Instituut.

THE ENGLISH LORD

*A*n English lord lived in a magnificent estate in the countryside, but on the weekends he often visited his club in London. First he ate there, then he drank too much, and finally he slept there overnight.

After such an evening of heavy drinking at the club, he called home from London the next morning with a huge hangover. The butler picked up the telephone.

"Hello James, milord here, go tell milady that I am still at the club and that I'll be home in about half an hour. I'll hold on."

A few moments later James returned to the telephone and said, "I just walked into milady's room, and I caught her in bed with the gardener."

"Damn, James," the lord said. "Go to the wine cellar, get my shotgun, and blow them to smithereens. I'll hold on."

Some time later the lord heard two dull bangs and James returned to the telephone. "I've killed them both, milord. What shall I do with the bodies?"

"Just chuck them in the swimming pool."

"But milord," James said, "we don't have a swimming pool."

The lord said, "Oh sorry, wrong number."

This joke was told in the first series of a Dutch television program called *Moppentoppers* (top jokers), RTL4, September–October 1994. It has not been published before (archives Meertens Instituut and Folktale Database).

THE TAPEWORM

A man, who was very skinny indeed although he ate like a pig, finally went to the doctor because his wife urged him to.

"Doctor, I think I may be suffering from a tapeworm."

The doctor looked at the miserable patient in a doubtful way and said, "Please, lie down on the examination couch."

The doctor took a small flashlight and examined the man's behind.

"Well, sir, this calls for a drastic approach."

The physician walked to the back room, and after five minutes he returned with an apple and a biscuit. Using some force, the doctor shoved the apple up the man's backside, waited for five minutes, and then shoved up the biscuit as well.

"Right, sir, repeat this for a whole week and come back on Friday."

The man returned home with mixed feelings.

This better work, he thought. He strictly followed the recipe and repeated the procedure on a daily basis. The next Friday, he visited the doctor again.

"Well, sir, did all go well?" the physician asked.

"Yes, doctor," the man said, "but I haven't gained any weight at all!"

The doctor asked the man to lie down on the examination couch again.

"That's a good sign," the doctor reassured the patient. "Wait just a moment, I'll be back soon."

The doctor went into the back room again, and quite soon returned with an apple and . . . a baseball bat!

The patient turned somewhat pale and said, "Doctor, I . . . ."

The physician urged the man to remain calm. The doctor shoved the apple up the patient's rear end, sat down, and waited.

After five minutes, the tapeworm came out and said, "Hey mate! Where's my cookie?"

BANG!

This joke was published on the Internet (www.casemanet/~klundert/joke.htm) and collected by Anouk Siegenbeek van Heukelom on October 15, 1998, for the Dutch Folktale Database. It has been published in T. Meder, *De magische vlucht* (Amsterdam, 2000), pp. 256–257.

ADAM'S FAULT

*W*hen God created the universe, He made heaven, the stars, the earth, the plants, and the animals. And He created man. Man was called Adam.

One day God visited Adam and asked, "Hey, Adam, are you enjoying your stay in paradise?"

Adam looked up and said, "Yeah, sure, it's a beautiful place, and I've got a nice house and all . . . ."

"So what's the matter then?" God asked.

Adam said, "Well, the squirrel has a partner, the cow has a companion, the bee is not alone . . . and I would like to have a companion too, actually."

God said, "Oh, is that all? I've got a solution to that; it's called woman, it is incredibly good-looking, irresistible, sexy, smart, and it does everything for you. It takes care of you, it cleans up after you, it is good in bed, it makes sure your carpet slippers await you when you come home, it does your dirty laundry . . . you name it."

"Oh, boy," said Adam, "that sounds great. I would like that!"

Then God said, "Yeah, but it will cost you. To be more precise, it will cost you an arm, a leg, and a ball."

Adam was startled by these demands and asked if he could sleep on it.

The next day, God returned and asked Adam if he had reached a decision yet.

"Yes," Adam replied. "What can I get for a rib?"

This joke was told in Amsterdam by student Elise de Bree on November 24, 1998. The translation is based on T. Meder, *De magische vlucht* (Amsterdam, 2000), p. 131.

AFTER CREATION

*A*fter creation, God wandered over the world and looked in admiration at what He had made. He came to Mongolia, and the Mongols made a respectful bow to Him and complimented Him on this creation. He went to Egypt, and all the Egyptians threw themselves into the dust of the desert and thanked Him on their bare knees. He kept on walking for a while and entered the Netherlands. Suddenly, He had arrived in the province of Groningen. An inhabitant of Groningen approached Him and yelled, "Oi, God, bugger off me property, and fast, will ye!"

This translation is based on Adjiedj Bakas and Hetty van Wolde, *Gluren bij de buren* (Lelystad, 1997), p. 32.

NASREDDIN HODJA

*N*asreddin Hodja was travelling through the country with his son. Nasreddin Hodja was sitting on the donkey, and his son walked right beside them. At a certain moment they entered a small village.

"It's a disgrace, it's a disgrace," the people said. "That man is comfortably sitting on a donkey, while his poor little son has to walk."

So Nasreddin Hodja decided to make a change. He put his son on the donkey, while he went on foot himself. After a while, they arrived at the next village.

"It's a disgrace, it's a disgrace," the people said. "The boy is sitting on the donkey and his poor old father has to walk."

So Nasreddin Hodja and his son decided to sit on the donkey together. As they came into the next village, they turned out to be all wrong again.

"It's a disgrace, it's a disgrace," the people said. "That poor donkey nearly collapses under the load of these two men."

Now Nasreddin and his son had no alternative left but for both to walk alongside the donkey. Again they arrived in another village.

"Are they crazy, or what?" the people said. "They have a donkey, but no one is riding it!"

One thing became perfectly clear to Nasreddin Hodja: Whatever you do, in the eyes of other people you can't do anything right.

This and other Nasreddin Hodja tales came to the Netherlands from the 1960s onwards, along with the Turkish immigrants. The story is a version of the international tale type ATU 1215, *The Miller, his Son, and the Donkey; Trying to Please Everyone*. The story was told in Utrecht (Utrecht) to me on October 28, 1998, by the young Dutch woman Nadia Eversteijn, who studied Turkish language and culture in Tilburg (North Brabant). The translation is based on T. Meder, *De magische vlucht* (Amsterdam, 2000), p. 243.

Part 10

FORMULA TALES

IT WAS NIGHT

*I*t was night, it was night, it was a pitch-dark night.

Seven robbers were sitting in the shadow of a blade of grass.

The leader said: "I say, Piet, tell us a story."

And Piet started:

"It was night, it was night, it was a pitch-dark night.

Seven robbers were sitting in the shadow of a blade of grass.

The leader said: "I say, Piet, tell us a story."

And Piet started:

"It was night, it was night, it was a pitch-dark night . . . ."

This repetitive formula tale is internationally known as folktale type ATU 2013, *"There was once a woman; the woman had a son."* This (unpublished) version was told to me by storyteller Heleen Kooij in Baarn (Utrecht) on November 10, 1998.

THE OLD WOMAN AND HER PIG

*A*n old woman sweeps the floor and finds a wooden penny.

She goes to the market and buys a pig, but the pig refuses to walk home.

She goes to the dog.

"Dog, will you bite the pig?

Pig won't go home."

"No," said the dog.

She goes to the stick.

"Stick, will you beat the dog?

Dog won't bite the pig,

Pig won't go home."

"No," said the stick.

She goes to the fire.

"Fire, will you burn the stick?

Stick won't beat the dog,

Dog won't bite the pig,

Pig won't go home."

"No," said the fire.

She goes to the water.

"Water, will you put out the fire?

Fire won't burn the stick,

Stick won't beat the dog,

Dog won't bite the pig,

Pig won't go home."

"No," said the water.

She goes to the ox.

"Ox, will you drink the water?

Water won't put out the fire,

Fire won't burn the stick,

Stick won't beat the dog,

Dog won't bite the pig,

Pig won't go home."

"No," said the ox.

She goes to the rope.

"Rope, will you hang the ox?

Ox won't drink the water,

Water won't put out the fire,

Fire won't burn the stick,

Stick won't beat the dog,

Dog won't bite the pig,

Pig won't go home."

"No," said the rope.

She goes to the rat.

"Rat, will you gnaw the rope?

Rope won't hang the ox,

Ox won't drink the water,

Water won't put out the fire,

Fire won't burn the stick,

Stick won't beat the dog,

Dog won't bite the pig,

Pig won't go home."

"Yes," said the rat.

The rope thinks, "I'm not crazy, I'd rather hang the ox."

The ox thinks, "I'd better drink the water."

The water thinks, "I'd better put out the fire."

The fire thinks, "I'd better burn the stick."

The stick thinks, "I'd better beat the dog."

The dog thinks, "I'd better bite the pig."

And there they went: the rat after the rope, the rope after the ox, the ox after the water, the water after the fire, the fire after the stick, the stick after the dog, the dog after the pig: The pig runs into the pigsty and the woman locks the door with a padlock.

This formula tale has been found in many variations in the Netherlands. It belongs to the international folktale type ATU 2030, *The old woman and her pig*. This particular version was sent to collector G. J. Boekenoogen on January 31, 1894, by Mrs. Cato P.E. de Hall from Oostwoud (North Holland). The translation is based on T. Meder and C. Hendriks, *Vertelcultuur in Nederland* (Amsterdam, 2005), pp. 153–154.

THE JAPANESE STONECUTTER

*A*long time ago and far away in the country of Japan, there lived a poor hard-working stonecutter in the mountains. His assignment was to keep the road through the mountains passable. That's why he was busy with his pickaxe day in, day out. The pieces he cut off from the rocks he used again to repair the holes in the road.

It was hard labour; the road through the mountains was long and there were always a lot of travellers: simple farmers taking their cattle to the market, millers with heavily packed donkeys, and distinguished travellers in magnificent vehicles.

Every time such a wealthy nobleman passed by, the stonecutter turned sad and sighed, while he bashed the rocks with mighty blows of his pickaxe.

Once, on a hot day in midsummer, a long procession of handsomely dressed people passed by, with a palanquin* in their midst. Next to this coach six servants walked, who had to attend to all the nobleman's wishes.

The stonecutter watched the procession move along, while he wiped off the sweat from his face with an old piece of cloth.

"Oh dear," he complained. "Such a king is being carried, and is given cool drinks, and I have to perform this slave's labour under a burning sun. I wish I were that king! At least, he has power over things."

The travellers slowly disappeared into the distance, and as the stonecutter was about to cut the rocks again, all of a sudden, a deep rumbling sound came from the hills. The man looked around and expected to see some thunderclouds. The sky was clear and dry, though. The man became scared: "Could it have been an earthquake?"

There was no evidence for that, because the ground did not shake, and the mountains just stood there like they had stood for thousands of years, indestructible by whatever force.

Still, to his amazement, the stonecutter heard the rumbling sound come closer and closer. The sound grew stronger and, all of a sudden, there was a voice, "What do I hear? Are you dissatisfied with your existence?"

The stonecutter trembled with fear, because he could not locate the source of the voice. It seemed to come from everywhere around him.

"I'm the mountain spirit," the dark voice said. "I see what you see and I hear what you hear. Are you dissatisfied with your existence?" repeated the voice of the mountain spirit.

The stonecutter stammered some kind of answer. "Uhhh, uhhh, oh well, . . . yes actually."

Thundering and even louder than before, the mountain spirit replied, "Then I can help you!"

The sky was clear and there sounded a thunderclap; the stonecutter felt as if a giant hand lifted him from the ground and carried him through the air. It happened so fast that everything around him faded, and he actually didn't dare to look; he tightly squeezed his eyes shut in fear.

All of a sudden, he was thrown down.

The stonecutter braced himself for a fall on the hard and rocky soil, but instead he landed on something soft and even. With his eyes still closed, the stonecutter touched the surroundings with his fingers. At the same time, it felt like he was sitting in a boat or a palanquin. There sounded a voice again, but this time much softer and lovelier than that of the mountain spirit.

"Did you sleep well, master?"

Slowly but softly he opened his eyes. He looked around; it was a palanquin!

The voice came from a girl sitting opposite to him; she was a geisha.

Her soft hand swept his sweaty forehead with a silk cloth. Now the stonecutter realized what had happened. After all, he had grumbled when the distinguished procession passed and he had said, "Let me be the king." Then the mountain spirit came and he said, "I can help you!" So now he was the king for real.

It was no dream, but he wondered if he really had the power of a king now.

"I am thirsty, give me something to drink," he said.

Almost immediately, a servant bowed through the curtain of the palanquin and poured out a cold drink in a beautifully decorated cup. Another servant waved a palm leaf to keep him cool. From that moment on, the stonecutter, who became king, exercised his power well. He only had to snap his fingers to put things in motion. The king enjoyed it. He was the most powerful man on earth. Nobody and nothing could achieve more than he. That's to say . . . . He noticed that sometimes things happened against his will. If it was very hot, the land dried out, the people did not go to work, and it looked like time stood still. The sun was to blame for that!

As he travelled in his palanquin on a hot day along the shriveled-up acres, he cursed the power of the sun. "Oh dear," he complained, "this sun keeps on shining and shining, and even a king remains powerless. I'm the boss, so let me be the sun!"

He closed his eyes to take a nap, when suddenly there was this rumbling sound in the hills again. He bent over to look outside where the thunderstorm would come from, but the sky appeared to be clear and dry all over.

He became afraid. "Could it be an earthquake?"

However, the bearers and the servants trudged on calmly, there was nothing out of the ordinary to see, the ground did not shake, and the mountains stood there like they had stood for thousands of years, indestructible by whatever force. Suddenly, the king who used to be stonecutter realized that this all had happened once before.

"What do I hear? Are you dissatisfied with your existence? I am the mountain spirit," said the dark voice. "I see what you see and I hear what you hear. Are you dissatisfied with your existence?" the voice of the mountain spirit repeated.

The king was actually quite happy; only the sun was mightier than he was. He stammered something like, "Uhhh, uhhh, well . . . no, not really."

The mountain spirit did not seem to hear him, though, and he roared, "Then I can help you!"

The sky was clear and a thunderclap sounded. Again, the king who once was a stonecutter had the feeling of being lifted and carried through the air by a gigantic hand. It went so fast that everything started to fade. Once more, he closed his eyes, because he was too frightened to look.

All of a sudden, he experienced complete peace and quiet around him. The sweet scent of wealth and power was gone. He opened his eyes and what he saw was totally new to him; he seemed to have entered a whole new world. There was nothing around him, only in the distance something round was hanging in the air. He didn't understand it at all and wanted to scratch himself behind the ears, but his hands were gone. Surely, he wasn't a king anymore. He gazed at the sphere in front of him and noticed that he could distinguish more and more details. He saw that the sphere was nothing else than the world and he could even see the people. They held hands before their eyes and looked up at him in agony. They were farmers standing near their burned acres. Were they looking at him?

The stonecutter, who once was granted to be king, had become the sun now!

He had complained and said, "Let me be the sun!"

The spirit of the mountain had heard him and said, "I can help you!"

The sun ruled over the entire world; he was able to grow food, but to burn it as well. The sun, who once was king, who once was a stonecutter, could be content. He sent his rays of sunshine where he liked and enjoyed the power he could exercise. That's to say . . . . He noticed that not everything went the way he wanted under certain circumstances. For a few summers now, his work was spoiled by sudden showers of rain and cold gusts of wind. The wind was to blame! So the sun complained and grumbled, "What's my power worth, if others can make fun of me? Let me be wind and storm!"

While the sun intended to send some scorching rays to the desert, suddenly a huge thundering came from the earth. The thunder changed into a loud voice that roared, "What do I hear? Are you dissatisfied with your existence? I am the mountain spirit," the dark voice continued. "I still can see what you see, and I still hear what you hear. Are you discontent with your life?" the voice of the mountain spirit repeated.

The sun had experienced this before and understood that this was his chance to become even more powerful. On former occasions he had been frightened, but not this time. The mountain spirit roared, "Then I can help you!"

The sun, who once was king, who once was a stonecutter, was prepared for anything, but nothing happened . . . . Or did it?

The world was turning very fast. It took a while before he realized that it was not the world that was moving fast, but he himself was racing over the face of the earth. He was the wind, he was the storm! Now he would let the world know he was there; at the most unexpected moments he could blow everything upside down. He could be a warm little breeze in spring, but he could be a storm in fall as well, tearing trees from the earth.

The wind, who once was the sun, who once was king, who once was a stonecutter, battered and roared, blew and whistled, and was content. Nothing could stop him, nothing could harm him. Season after season he just did his job.

Still, he was unable to be completely satisfied. There were things that seemed to laugh at his raging power. There were mountains, for instance, that stood on this world like they had stood for thousands of years, indestructible by whatever force. Even as a hurricane, the wind was powerless. So he complained and grumbled and now he called the mountain spirit himself, "What's keeping you? I thought you would come and help me!"

The wind, who once was the sun, who once was king, who once was a stonecutter, waited for the rumbling sound coming towards him to help him.

Something was rumbling all right, not outside, but inside him the thunder could be heard. There was no voice this time; that wasn't necessary. He himself became the being in the rocks, the ghost of the stones all over the world, of the mountains and the hills; he had become the spirit of the mountain!

No need to think any more—unchanging, motionless, permanent—stone remained stone . . . .

No need to think any more—unchanging, motionless, permanent—stone remained stone . . . .

No need to think any more—unchanging, motionless, permanent—stone remained stone . . . .

No need to think any more—unchanging, motionless, permanent—stone remained stone . . . .

A long time ago and far away in the country of Japan, there lived a poor hardworking stonecutter in the mountains. His assignment was to keep the road through the mountains passable. That's why he was busy with his pickaxe day in, day out. He cut off pieces from the rocks . . . .

---

*A litter (vehicle); a carriage without wheels for transport of persons.

This formula tale is a version of ATU 2031, *Stronger and strongest*. It became known in the Netherlands thanks to the Dutch author Eduard Douwes Dekker (1820–1887; aka Multatuli), who incorporated the tale in his famous novel *Max Havelaar* (1860). The story belongs to the repertoire of professional storyteller Rens de Vette, who lives in Arnhem (Gelderland) but was born in Vlaardingen (South Holland) in 1955. He sent the tale via e-mail to the Meertens Instituut on January 12, 2005, adding that he regularly told the story to groups of adolescents, especially during religious meetings. The theme of such meetings is often "Being Who You Are." The translation is based on the (unpublished) e-mail (archives Meertens Instituut and Dutch Folktale Database).

THE THOUSANDTH BAR
OF SOAP

"*A* truck with a load of soap was driving along a small road. All of a sudden, the truck skidded and turned over. The entire load scattered on the road. The driver was angry, because he had to pick up all these bars of soap and put them in the truck again. In the end he had gathered them all but one. Where was that thousandth bar of soap?"

[Listener:] "I don't know."

"Neither do I. Hmm, that's perhaps a bit silly. Let me tell you something else. A man and a woman were sitting in the train. The man carried an umbrella and the woman had a little lap dog. The little dog started to yap like mad all of a sudden. The man became extremely annoyed, but the woman didn't do a thing about it. At a certain point, the man was fed up with it. He stood up and threw the little dog right out of the window. The woman was furious, took the man's umbrella and threw it out of the window as well. At the next station, they both got off. On the platform, they looked into the direction they came from. A short while later, they saw the dog come running. Guess what he had in his mouth?"

[Listener:] "Well, the umbrella . . . ?"

"No, that thousandth bar of soap!"

This (unpublished) version of ATU 2204, *The dog's cigar*, was sent to me via e-mail on February 24, 2002, by Floris Koot.

SOURCES AND FURTHER READING

Aarne, A., and S. Thompson,: *The Types of the Folktale: A Classification and Bibliography*. Helsinki, 1964. (FFC 184)

Bakas, A., and H. van Wolde. *Gluren bij de buren. Humor en diversiteit*. Lelystad, 1997.

Blécourt, W. de. *Volksverhalen uit Nederlands Limburg*. Utrecht and Antwerp, 1981.

———. *Volksverhalen uit Noord-Brabant*. Utrecht and Antwerp, 1980.

Boekenoogen, G. J. "Nederlandsche sprookjes en vertelsels." *Volkskunde* 15 (1903): 114–115.

———. "Nederlandsche sprookjes en vertelsels." *Volkskunde* 17 (1905): 103–106.

Brunvand, J. H. *The Baby Train and Other Lusty Urban Legends*. New York, 1994.

Burger, P. *De wraak van de kangoeroe*. Amsterdam, 1993.

Cohen, J. *Nederlandse Volksverhalen*. Zutphen, 1952.

Damen, John. "De sage van de Witte Wieven." *Kampioen* 118, no. 1 (January 2003): 62–64.

Dekker, T., J. van der Kooi, and T. Meder. *Van Aladdin tot Zwaan Kleef Aan. Lexicon van sprookjes: ontstaan, ontwikkeling, variaties*. Nijmegen, 1997.

Dutch Folktale Database. Available at http://www.verhalenbank.nl.

Franke, S. *Legenden langs de Noordzee*. Zutphen, 1934.

Jong, E. de, and P. Klaasse. *Sagen en Legenden van de Lage Landen*. Bussum, 1980.

Jong, E. de, and H. Sleutelaar. *Sprookjes van de Lage Landen*. Amsterdam, 1996.

Koman, Ruben A. *Bèèh . . . ! Groot Dordts volksverhalenboek*. Bedum, 2005.

———. *Dalfser Muggen. Volksverhalen uit een Overijsselse gemeente*. Bedum, 2006.

Kooi, J. van der. *Van Janmaanje en Keudeldoemke. Groninger Sprookjesboek*. Groningen, 2003.

———. *Volksverhalen in Friesland. Lectuur en mondelinge overlevering. Een typencatalogus*. Groningen, 1984.

Meder, T. *De magische vlucht. Nederlandse volksverhalen uit de collectie van het Meertens Instituut.* Amsterdam, 2000.

———. *Vertelcultuur in Waterland. De volksverhalen uit de Collectie Bakker (ca. 1900).* Amsterdam, 2001.

Meder, T., and C. Hendriks. *Vertelcultuur in Nederland. Volksverhalen uit de Collectie Boekenoogen (ca. 1900).* Amsterdam, 2005.

Meder, T., and M. van Dijk. *Doe open Zimzim. Verhalen en liedjes uit de Utrechtse wijk Lombok.* Amsterdam, 2000.

Meder, T., and E. Venbrux. "Authenticity as an Analytic Concept in Folkloristics: A Case of Collecting Folktales in Friesland." *Etnofoor* 17, nos. 1–2 (2004): 199–214.

———. "Vertelcultuur." In *Volkscultuur. Een inleiding in de Nederlandse etnologie.* Edited by T. Dekker, H. Roodenburg, and G. Rooijakkers, 282–336. Nijmegen, 2000.

Poortinga, Y. *De foet fan de reinbôge. Fryske folksforhalen.* Baarn, 1979.

Portnoy, E. *Broodje Aap.* 10th ed. Amsterdam, 1992.

Sinninghe, J. R. W. *Katalog der niederländischen Märchen-, Ursprungssagen-, Sagen- und Legendenvarianten.* Helsinki, 1943.

———. *Spokerijen in Amsterdam en Amstelland.* Zaltbommel, 1975.

———. *Spokerijen in de Zaanstreek en Waterland.* Zaltbommel, 1975.

———. *Volkssprookjes uit Nederland en Vlaanderen.* Den Haag, 1978.

Sliggers, B. *Volksverhalen uit Noord- en Zuid-Holland.* Utrecht and Antwerp, 1980.

Stuiveling, G., ed. *Esopet.* Amsterdam, 1965.

Uther, H.-J. *Types of International Folktales. A Classification and Bibliography, Based on the System of Antti Aarne and Stith Thompson.* Helsinki, 2004. (FFC 284-286)

Venbrux, E., and T. Meder. "Anders Bijma's Folktale Repertoire and Its Collectors." *Fabula* 40, nos. 3/4 (1999): 259–277.

INDEX

ABOUT THE AUTHOR

Dr. Theo Meder studied Dutch language and literature at the University of Leyden. Since 1994 he has been working as a folk narrative researcher at the Department of Ethnology at the Meertens Institute in Amsterdam. He has published books and articles on fairy tales, traditional legends, jokes, riddles, contemporary legends, and personal narratives. He is currently a senior researcher and manager of the Dutch Folktale Database (www.verhalenbank.nl) as well as at the DOC Volksverhaal, the center for documentation and research on folktales in the Netherlands (www.docvolksverhaal.nl).

Recent Titles in the
World Folklore Series

Folktales from the Japanese Countryside
As told by Hiroko Fujita; Edited by Fran Stallings with Harold Wright and Miki Sakurai

Mayan Folktales; Cuentos folklóricos Mayas
Retold and Edited by Susan Conklin Thompson, Keith Thompson, and Lidia López de López

The Flower of Paradise and Other Armenian Tales
Translated and Retold by Bonnie C. Marshall; Edited and with a Foreword by Virginia Tashjian

The Magic Lotus Lantern and Other Tales from the Han Chinese
Haiwang Yuan

Brazilian Folktales
Livia de Almeida and Ana Portella; Edited by Margaret Read MacDonald

The Seven Swabians, and Other German Folktales
Anna Altmann

English Folktales
Edited by Dan Keding and Amy Douglas

The Snow Maiden and Other Russian Tales
Translated and Retold by Bonnie C. Marshall; Edited by Alla V. Kulagina

From the Winds of Manguito: Cuban Folktales in English and Spanish (Desde los vientos de Manguito: Cuentos folklóricos de Cuba, en inglés y español)
Retold by Elvia Perez; Edited by Margaret Read MacDonald

Tales from the Taiwanese
Retold by Gary Marvin Davison

Indonesian Folktales
Retold by Murti Bunanta; Edited by Margaret Read MacDonald

Folktales from Greece: A Treasury of Delights
Retold by Soula Mitakidou, Anthony L. Manna with Melpomeni Kanatsouli

Additional titles in this series can be found at www.lu.com